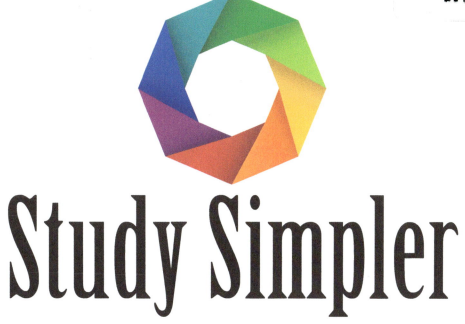

Study Simpler

STUDY SKILLS DEVELOPMENT

MITCH COLVER

❧ 2013 ❧

MITCH COLVER

www.studysimpler.com

Cover image is a derivative of "*Rainbow Colors*" by OpenClips, adapted for commercial use under license CC0 1.0.
http://pixabay.com/en/rainbow-colors-colors-spectrum-153229/

First Edition, December 2013

COLVER, MITCH
Washington: 2013
1st ed. Hardcover
ISBN-13: 978-0-615-95513-1
ISBN-10: 0615955134
EDUCATION; STUDY SKILLS; TUTORING; UNIVERSITY; RESOURCES

To all of the wonderful students and dedicated employees that have inspired me over the past seven years, especially those who convinced me to finally write all of this down.

Contents

Introduction
Starting Simpler

i.   Starting Simpler ❧ 11
ii.   The Need for an Organized Approach ❧ 13
iii. The Helping Professional as a Guide ❧ 14
iv.   Using the Model ❧ 16
v.   Providing an Experience ❧ 17

Chapter I
Study Space

i.   Place Cells ❧ 23
ii.   Avoiding Distractions ❧ 24
iii. Relocation ❧ 25
iv.   Productive Ambiance ❧ 26
v.   Music & Mood ❧ 27

Chapter II
Study Intervals

i.   Take a Break ❧ 31
ii.   Review Often ❧ 32
iii. "Personal Time Survey" ❧ 33
iv.   Engram Maintenance ❧ 34
v.   Tracking Progress ❧ 35
vi.   Course Attendance ❧ 36
vii. Homework and Reading ❧ 37
viii. Seek Resources Early and Often ❧ 38

Chapter III
Study Method

i.   Individual Differences ❧ 41
ii.   Multiple Intelligences ❧ 42
iii. Bloom's Taxonomy ❧ 43
iv.   Notetaking Skills ❧ 44
v.   Managing Test Anxiety ❧ 45
vi.   Active Listening ❧ 46
vii. Organizational Skills ❧ 47
viii. Fluency and Speed ❧ 48

Chapter IV
Study People

i.   Introversion vs. Extraversion ❧ 51
ii.   Social Influence ❧ 52
iii. Teach to Learn ❧ 53
iv.   Supplemental Instruction ❧ 54
v.   Get to Know Your Professors ❧ 55
vi.   Building a Community of Support ❧ 56

Chapter V
Study Loyalty

i.   Having a Positive Attitude ❧ 59
ii.   "The Hidden Power of Smiling" ❧ 60
iii. Victim vs. Creator ❧ 61
iv.   Maslow's Hierarchy ❧ 62
v.   Atkinson's Model of Motivation ❧ 63
vi.   Motivation Styles ❧ 64
vii. Motivational Barriers ❧ 65
viii. Grow Your Intelligence ❧ 66
ix.   All Diplomas Look the Same ❧ 67
x.   Fixed Mindset vs. Growth Mindset ❧ 68

Chapter VI
Study Energy

i.   Glucose & Self-Regulation ❧ 71
ii. Fuel Proper Study Habits ❧ 72
iii. Uncertainty and Energy Levels ❧ 73
iv. The Myth About Coffee & Energy Drinks ❧ 74
v.   Sleep ❧ 76
vi. Dreams ❧ 77

Chapter VII
Study Resources

i.   Writers' Center ❧ 81
ii.   Disability Support Services ❧ 81
iii. Career Services ❧ 82
iv.   TRiO Advising & McNair Scholars ❧ 82
v.   Counseling Services ❧ 83
vi.   Tutoring ❧ 83
vii. khanacademy.org ❧ 84
viii. Online Tutoring ❧ 84
ix.   Academic Software ❧ 84

Chapter VIII
The Tutor Guide

i.   The Tutor Guide ❧ 87
ii.   Self-Efficacy ❧ 88
iii. Social Intelligence vs. Pedagogy ❧ 89
iv.   Modeling Coping with Ignorance ❧ 90
v.   Three Magic Questions ❧ 91
vi.   Gradual Release of Responsibility ❧ 92
vii. Vgotsky's Zone of Proximal Development ❧ 93
viii. A Metaphor for Success ❧ 94
ix.   Seven Stages of a Productive Tutoring Session ❧ 96

Origins of the word *student* date back to a 14th century French term meaning "one who is studying" and even further back to Latin origins that refer to "painstaking application of oneself" to some endeavor. This rich conceptual heritage of what it means to be a student presents itself in stark contrast to the popular modern definition of the word, listed in Merriam-Webster: "a person who attends a school, college, or university"[1] or, in other words, just showing up. This philosophical shift, from emphasizing the effortful nature of the role that students fulfill to merely emphasizing enrollment, illustrates one of the most striking realities of the modern post-secondary education system: students enter the realm of higher-education with a huge array of personal differences in how prepared they are to actually be students. To be more accurate, the importance of this preparation is not so much in how individuals approach *student-being*, but rather and more importantly, in how they approach *student-doing*. For our purposes, we can shorten *student-doing* to *student-ing*, or perhaps even more simply, to *studying*.

In general, unless effective study skills happen to have been acquired and internalized during earlier educational experiences, students entering institutions of higher education can quickly find their personal portfolio of study skills ill-suited for rigorous course content. Unfortunately, students who begin to struggle with university-level course material often mistakenly conclude that their challenges arise exclusively from issues they are having with the course material itself. Too often, many fail to realize that their struggle may actually extend from challenges they are having with *studying* the course material. In other words, Jonny's real problem isn't calculus... it's *studying* calculus that he can't get the hang of.

While this may seem like a purely semantic distinction, helping-professionals who have spent a considerable amount of time working with students typically understand the idea that, more than the course material and concepts, poor study habits are at the root of many of the difficulties that students face. Missing class, failing to complete assignments, neglecting to read through the text, and a refusal to interact with the professor outside of the classroom are only a few examples of a litany of inadequate study habits that plague students' academic lives. Overcoming these challenges through effective acquisition and implementation of study skills is critical to students' ability to maintain sufficient academic progress and, more importantly, to ultimately persist and graduate.

In response to this widespread need for study skills development, universities and colleges actively provide a myriad of academic support services, which are designed to bridge the gap between where each student happens to be and where they need to be in order to achieve success. Characteristically, the two main services provided at institutions of higher education to improve study skills have been workshops and first-year experience courses, which are well-known to positively impact student well-being as often as they are implemented effectively. These courses and workshops can and should be the first line of defense against epidemically underdeveloped study skills amongst students, however, certain limitations to their effective implementation are something that institutions are still working to overcome.

For example, while assigning students to attend a typical study skills course or workshop may be possible in many situations, there may also be problematic instances in which students' busy lives or credit loads will not allow them to access and benefit from such services. Indeed, many of the students who require the greatest amount of study skills development, as Vincent Tinto points out in his book *Completing College*, tend to be the very students whose busy schedules prevent them from participating in any university service outside of simply attending their classes.[2] Additionally, there are other problematic instances in which students have been encouraged or even required to attend study skills courses or workshops, but fail to attend or fully engage the services due to a poor sense of self-efficacy relative to study habits. They neither believe that they will perform well in the process of acquiring study skills, nor are willing to expose themselves to the vulnerabilities of making the attempt.

In other situations, study skills courses and workshops are utilized by students but, for a variety of reasons, produce less than desirable results. Often, such outcomes are neither the fault of the instructor nor the students, as study skills development is such a personally nuanced process that some of the best tips and strategies may not work for everyone. Indeed, acquiring effective study skills often involves incorporating new behaviors and strategies into preexisting styles of academic engagement that have been ingrained over the course of a lifetime. As a result, a single study skills workshop or course designed to appeal to a wide audience of students may end up being less effective for certain students than originally intended.

In light of these realities and a continued need to offer dynamic solutions to the spectrum of issues that students face in the area of study skills development, *Study Simpler* was written with the belief that study skills development can be broken down into a model of brief, engaging interventions that can be personally tailored by helping-professionals to dovetail nicely with each student's academic individuality. The acronym *SIMPLER* was devised as a means of providing continuity to the model through an easy to remember mnemonic that covers seven holistic domains of student success: *Space, Intervals, Method, People, Loyalty, Energy,* and *Resources*. As shown in the table on the following page, these seven categories make up the *Who, What, When, Where, Why,* and *How* of studying.

Academic well-being, like so many other aspects of our lives, is so intrinsically connected to countless other areas of our functioning that attempting to compartmentalize the academic-self is essentially futile. Environmental influences, social distractions, and physiological considerations are just a small start to the list of influences that can make or break a student's academic career. The holistic philosophy of *Study Simpler* extends directly from this recognition that, like a car engine, students have many complexly interconnected components that must work in concert to achieve momentum.

STUDY SIMPLER		
S ↝ Space		Where is the student choosing to study?
I ↝ Intervals		When and how frequently does the student study?
M ↝ Method		How does the student approach the material?
P ↝ People		Who does the student interact with while studying?
L ↝ Loyalty		Why is the student motivated to be loyal to their studies?
E ↝ Energy		How does the student fuel their study habits?
R ↝ Resources		What resources does the student choose to access?

Within these seven main categories, each of which comprises the contents of an entire chapter within this book (Chapters 1-7), fifty-two different topics are discussed to provide a snapshot of relevant and effective principles of academic engagement. To add ease of use, each page of chapters 1-7 covers a single topic that can be effectively read, understood, and discussed in a roughly five minute period of time and used to infuse systemic vitality into the lives of students.

Simplifying study skills development using this more holistic approach allows study skills interventions to be more effectively embedded within a broad range of services throughout the university. Due to the adaptive and interpersonal nature of *Study Simpler*, the interventions are suitable for use in any number of settings, including lectures, advising appointments, mentoring sessions, tutoring sessions, residence hall meetings, chapter meetings, orientation classes, athletic advising appointments, leadership seminars, and supplemental instruction groups.

Rather than supplanting more formalized approaches to study skills development, this model seeks to supplement study skills courses and workshops by encouraging and empowering helping-professionals across campus to embrace the opportunity to embed study skills development within the services, programs, and courses that they are responsible for implementing. In doing so, these helping-professionals simultaneously become stakeholders in a culture of study skills development that can transform both institutions and the students they serve.

The Need for an Organized Approach

Study Simpler relies on a threefold-approach that recognizes and attempts to address some of the major underlying realities of why students tend to struggle so much with study skills development:

1. *Interpersonal* - While *Study Simpler* is well suited for use by college students who happen to be motivated to develop study skills on their own, the plain reality is that most students will not attempt to develop more effective study skills without encouragement from some kind of knowledgeable helping figure. This individual can be a parent, mentor, friend, or any of the numerous helping-professionals found within post-secondary education. If study skills development is attached, in the mind of the students, to a caring and compassionate individual, those study skills are far more likely to be used in a meaningful, effective manner.

2. *Intriguing* - In a world of social media, high definition experiences, and an endless supply of aesthetically vibrant entertainment available at a moment's notice, students are more susceptible than ever to disengaging from any situation that does not effectively engage their interest and attention. These realities demand that study skills development be presented in a way that relies on intriguing information and research that students may have never heard before. Information and ideas that reframe study skills in a unique and interesting way help to achieve what Howard Gardner has called "Representational Redescriptions," which allow individuals to see a familiar problem from a completely new perspective.[3] This perspective helps students to experience a sense that the discussion of study skills has, in fact, exposed them to a new way of doing things, rather than providing them with tired old advice.

3. *Individualized* - Study skills development must resonate with each student's personal experiences in order to be seen as valuable and needed. Unless any given discussion of study skills acknowledges each student's unique palette of strengths, as well as their personal struggles and challenges, there is no guarantee that the students will even attempt to incorporate new found skill sets into their preexisting strategies. In order to facilitate this kind of individualized support, helping-professionals can rely on the rapport they have already built with each student to inform their selection of which *Study Simpler* topic will most effectively meet each student's needs during each discussion.

Helping-professionals that use the model to assist the students that they serve should realize that, in all reality, their own ongoing interaction with the student *is* what will impact and facilitate each student's progress. *Study Simpler* was written to provide brief and meaningful strategies that can make a big difference in the lives of students, but the relationship that exists and that is maintained between the student and the helping-professional, in addition to the insight that this relationship provides to the helping professional as they individualize study skills discussions, is key to the growth that *Study Simpler* was designed to facilitate.

The Helping Professional as a Guide

While it would seem intuitive for *Study Simpler* to have been written directly to students, the information was instead crafted with particular attention to an audience of—for lack of a better term—*helping-professionals*. The interesting and often overlooked truth about study skills manuals (including this one!) is that students who are in need of study skills development rarely have the capacity or interest to actually open the pages of a text written about the topic of study skills. Many of the books that are available are hundreds of pages in length, include huge sections of prose that bleed from one page to the next, and contain a variety of images and charts that punctuate the material in a textbook-like manner. If the point of the book is to impart effective study skills, why does their design so often require those skills as a prerequisite for accessing the material?

As a direct response to these less effective study skills guides, *Study Simpler* was written to enable helping-professionals to serve as living, compassionate, and interpersonal insulators between students and the study skills development that is so necessary to their success. Helping-professionals not only have the capacity to intuit the needs of such students, but also to filter out all but the most critical information that each student needs in order to be successful. This dynamic, interactive, and considerate *exchange* between helping-professionals and students is what makes the *Simpler* model work.

In the broadest sense, helping-professionals as a category includes, but is not limited to, any member of the institutional community that would conceivably find themselves in a one-on-one or small group advising or mentoring session or meeting with students. Although the term helping-professionals predominantly refers to career level practitioners in higher education, student employees that work in helping roles can benefit just as greatly, if not more so, from the use of *Study Simpler,* as well. Examples of helping-professionals that could benefit from using *Study Simpler* with their students include:

Learning Resource Center Staff	Faculty
Academic Coaches	Student Affairs Staff
Teaching Assistants	Supplemental Instruction Facilitators
Community & Residential Advisors	Learning Community Mentors
Academic Advisors	Peer Mentors
Tutors	Members of Student Government
Academic Specialists within Athletics	TRiO & McNair Advisors
Academic Chairs of Sororities and Fraternities	Other Special Programs Advisors

Helping-professionals from these categories, in addition to those not listed, who are willing to temporarily set aside their typical agenda with students in order to have a brief discussion of study skills immediately bridge the gap between these students and support that they may not be getting from other source. Compared to the often straightforward nature of making a course recommendation, issuing a referral to another campus resource, processing student paperwork or simply starting the day's lecture, engaging the topic of exactly what combination of study habits students might benefit from can easily seem overwhelming or even off-task. However, this type of holistic engagement, if done in a considerate and involving way, can have a drastic influence on the mindset of students. Having the feeling that at least one member of the institution is "in their corner" can easily make the difference between a student choosing to stay enrolled or, out of frustration, deciding to leave the institution entirely.

Additionally, students who experience interventions using *Study Simpler* will appreciate the attempts of the helping-professional to impart these skills in a way that is both personally attentive and non-time-consuming. In fact, the need for brevity and quickly-acquired familiarity with the recommended study skills is the reason that *Study Simpler* was deliberately written to be roughly one hundred pages in length. While many of the page-long sections within the manual can be read out loud in less than two minutes, using appropriate techniques of dialogue and inquiry as part of the *Simpler* model will extend and personalize the topics for each student during each discussion session. Building this kind of rapport and organic delivery of the material, through more than simply hashing through the words written on the page, will help students feel attended to, rather than processed through a standardized model.

Using the Model

In order to use *Study Simpler* most effectively with any particular student or group of students, the helping-professional should, in a fairly organic manner, decide which topic page will be discussed based on the students' current needs and challenges. The fifty-two skills and resources within the manual were not written to be addressed in any particular order. In fact, the *Simpler* model benefits from an element of spontaneity and flexibility, especially relative to dynamic nature of student lives.

Additionally, in the absence of any particularly concerning issue currently being faced by the students, the helping-professional may instead decide to select a topic page from *Study Simpler* that they suspect students would find particularly interesting and that would spark a particularly engaging discussion. Sharing this second type of intervention, in the absence of any pressing concern, is meant to provide continuity to the model (rather than simply skipping a session) and to help develop continued rapport between the helping-professional and students while simultaneously providing useful, life relevant information.

Identifying an appropriate intervention for each session, one that fits either the first or second category, can be accomplished by asking the following two questions:

1. Is there an immediately pressing concern or previously identified challenge that this student (or group of students) is currently facing, which could be effectively addressed by one of the many topics within *Study Simpler*?

2. In the absence of an immediately pressing concern or previously identified challenge, is there a topic that this student (or group of students) would find particularly interesting and that would help to build or maintain ongoing rapport?

Answering these questions might take a few moments of the helping-professional's time, but can be an important aspect to effectively tailoring each intervention to meet student needs. A sincere desire and consistent commitment to going through the motions of asking the questions before each and every session or meeting is critical to the effectiveness of the *Simpler* model. Setting aside time for this conscious, effortful moment of inquiry and reflection will result in an ongoing development of the internal, personal narrative that the helping-professional maintains about each of their students. This personal touch of purposeful consideration is an important aspect of what makes this model work.

To aid helping-professionals in the selection process, a guide entitled "Key Issues" has been included in the Appendix (page 99). This table contains categories of student struggles and several possible variations of each struggle along with a list of suggested topic pages that might help address those concerns. For example, in the category called "Student struggles with...", the identified issue of "... performing as well on the test as on their homework," refers the helping-professional to several topic pages, including one related to the importance of using practice tests. Practitioners that rely on this index will expedite the selection process and simultaneously become more familiar with the variety of topics available within *Study Simpler*.

A "Progress Tracking Sheet" has also been provided within the Appendix (page 107) and can be photocopied to assist helping-professionals keep track of which topics they have already covered with particular students or groups of students.

As a side note, in addition to the study skills and resources presented within these pages, there are a multitude of practical tips and well-thought-out pieces of advice not included that helping-professionals may already be familiar with. This type of personally identified topic can also be discussed with students as deemed appropriate by the helping-professional as part of the *Simpler* model. In fact, this is ideal, since personally identified topics will tend to be delivered in a more natural, sincere, and genuine manner.

Providing an Experience

As world-renowned psychologist Freida Fromm-Reichman eloquently observed, in order for individuals to experience true growth in life they need 'an experience, not an explanation.' In this same spirit, the *Study Simpler* model was designed with the understanding that students learn far more from educational environments that allow them to have experiences, rather than merely hearing explanations.

In order to facilitate this kind of meaningful experiential growth, discussions that use *Study Simpler* should involve both a presentation of one study skill or resource and the presentation of one or more *Discussion Questions, Action Items,* or *Follow-Ups*:

1. *Discussion Questions* are meant to encourage a two-way exchange of information, rather than a one-way, lecture style presentation. It is critical that discussion questions seem natural and that they are born of a real desire to listen to what students have to say about the topic.

2. *Action Items* are behaviors that the helping-professional can invite or encourage students to engage in, especially as a way of experimenting with the recommended study skills. Without a call to specific action, the *Simpler* model becomes predominantly cosmetic. Additionally, particularly dedicated helping-professionals who have already worked with *Study Simpler* have reported that engaging in the *Action Items* along with their students, as appropriate and possible, is not only a rewarding experience, but something that develops a sense of solidarity with their students relative to the process of study skills development.

3. *Follow-Ups* are critical to the effectiveness of the *Simpler* model because they reinforce the interpersonal nature of the interventions and allow both the student and helping-professional to evaluate the intervention's effectiveness, based on each student's experience. Additionally, when students expect to have to report on "how it's going," they are forced to think about their study skills habits in a self-reflective manner that is so critical to growth. *Follow-Ups* also serve to extend the discussion from one session to the next and provide continuity to the entire experience.

At the bottom of each topic page within *Study Simpler,* helping-professionals will find possible *Discussion Questions, Action Items,* and *Follow-Ups* that can be used directly or simply referred to in order to generate ideas for items that helping-professionals author themselves.

In an attempt to condense the contents of *Study Simpler* out of the interest of time, helping-professionals may intuitively try to combine two or more closely-related topics into a single session. While this may occasionally be desirable, care must be taken to prevent the student from becoming overwhelmed or inundated by too much information. Processing each topic page thoroughly and attentively using effective techniques of dialogue and inquiry results in a more organic and personable experience, rather than a brisk dispensation of one-size-fits-all knowledge.

In fact, to achieve the greatest outcomes, helping-professionals may find that the same topic may need to be revisited multiple times across three or four different sessions in order to provide the greatest level of support to students. Additionally, as students choose to set new goals related to each intervention, a following meeting's discussion should be devoted to revisiting those goals and topics, rather than moving on to discuss new topics. This should even be the norm, rather than the exception, as it sets the tone of an ongoing exchange, rather than a single instance of assistance.

In connection with these issues, the results of a recent survey that assessed the student experience of *Study Simpler* confirmed that student ratings of the model significantly increase when helping-professionals remain consistent in how frequently and how thoroughly they engage the interventions. Students who worked with helping-professionals that regularly engaged in interventions that involved more than just reading from the page consistently rated the model with high marks. These students reported having a pleasant experience with *Simpler* and indicated that the interventions were helping them in a holistic, rather than circumstantial, manner. Conversely, students who worked with helping-professionals who only engaged the model with minimal effort and at inconsistent intervals or with helping-professionals who tried to combine multiple interventions into single sessions indicated that using *Simpler* had not been that pleasant of an experience and did not have an impact on their academic proficiency.

These outcomes emphasize the importance of providing each student with a positive, ongoing, and personally-tailored *experience*. As a matter of style, each discussion may involve reading directly from the manual but, more desirably, can be less formal and simply use the content of each topic page as a reference point, rather than a script. The more familiar helping-professionals become with the topics presented in *Study Simpler*, the more readily they will be able to discuss the topics without referring to the written text. Since students react negatively to poorly implemented interventions, helping-professionals who engage in study skills development in a fun, entertaining, and even impromptu manner can actually insulate students from even noticing that study skills development is underway.

Regardless of individual differences that can and do exist between each helping-professional's style of delivery, all study skills discussions should feel natural and genuine. Helping-professionals should use enthusiasm and personal rapport as the cornerstone of any discussion about academic well-being. Helping-professionals should also feel empowered to engage the topic of academic engagement according to their own strengths, interests, and conversational style. Ultimately, any user of this model should feel confident in exercising their own judgment and proceed in a manner that is best suited to the challenges that they find their students are currently facing.

As a side note, Chapter 8 (*The Tutor Guide*) has been included to aid in the development of tutor pedagogy in connection with *Study Simpler*. In truth, any helping-professional who has ever found themselves assisting students with homework would benefit from consideration of this chapter, as it outlines methods of effectively engaging students in a manner that preserves their responsibility for the work. Many of the principles contained in Chapter 8 are just as relevant in teaching, mentoring, and advising sessions, as they are for tutoring sessions.

In whatever manner *Study Simpler* is utilized by helping-professionals, student success should always be central to the process and engaged from a standpoint of encouragement, holistic consideration, and relationship-focused growth and development.

Certain supporting materials, such as full-page worksheets, can be found on the resources page of *www.studysimpler.com*.

Chapter I
Study Space

Place Cells

Research shows that our minds orient themselves to the surrounding environment using cues given to us by our place cells. Place cells are individual neurons that are coded with information any time we are exposed to a new location.[1] These cells are subsequently maintained and strengthened through repeated exposure to those environments, which causes the cells to be more fully established and connected within the neural network of our mind. Upon entering any familiar environment, our associated place cells activate and cue our minds and bodies to prepare to engage in the same kind of activity that we engaged in the last time we were in that environment. For example, if we have spent a lot of time on a particular couch watching TV, then anytime we sit down on that couch our place cells will cue our mind and body to prepare to watch TV. Similarly, if we have spent a lot of time in a particular park playing frisbee, then going to that park will make us feel like playing frisbee. In this way, place cells have a powerful subconscious effect on our ability to function.

As far as study habits go, place cells become critical to understanding why certain environments are more conducive to productive study habits than others. With these concerns in mind, it is recommended that individuals find a previously unused space which can remain dedicated to productive study sessions and nothing else. Several locations may have to be tested or tried out before an individual finds one that works well, but the search is worth the final outcome. Once this study space has been established and is being used productively, individuals must be careful to safeguard their place cells from becoming polluted by conflicting activities. For example, if an individual takes a lot of breaks within this newly dedicated space to check social media, the space may inadvertently become a social media checking space as far as our place cells are concerned, rather than a study space. This type of study space pollution is common and highly destructive.

Wherever a student chooses to study, ensuring that it remains free from distractions and protected as a dedicated study space is critical to avoiding the inadvertently negative influence that place cells can have on productive study habits.

DISCUSSION QUESTION

❧ Have place cells influenced any of your study sessions that have been less productive?

ACTION ITEM

❧ Experiment by studying right in the middle of your favorite hangout and see what happens.

FOLLOW-UP

❧ Report the outcome of your experiment to a helping-professional you like and trust.

Avoiding Distractions

After learning about how place cells influence our ability to study (see previous page), it is also helpful to discuss some common distractions that can be pitfalls to maintaining a productive study space. Some obvious examples are studying in front of the TV or studying in bed. Both of these environments cue our mind to slowly shut down and disengage from the active mental state that is so crucial to productive study sessions. While studying in bed or on a big comfy couch may seem desirable, the diminishing returns are a quick path to poor retention of the material being studied. Our minds have to constantly resist the urge to give in to the comfortable surface by reorienting itself to the study session, which depletes mental energy. Similarly, studying in front of a TV causes our place cells to cue our minds away from our homework and back to the highly rewarding entertainment we are so used to experiencing when we sit there.

Exposing ourselves to such subconscious distractions is like stacking the deck against ourselves and against productive study habits, because, attempting to ignore such powerful distractions saps energy and is likely to result in the final outcome of transitioning away from the study session into a far less taxing activity like channel surfing or counting sheep.

Other distractions that our minds are especially sensitive to are social media and other instances of social distraction, as well as distracting bouts of hunger. Since our relationships with people are one of the most important aspects of our well-being (see page 52), our minds are easily cued away from studying in order to interact with family and friends. Similarly, because eating is so crucial to our well-being, our mind will rapidly shut down if unfueled. Ensuring that we have a healthy supply of snacks and water can make a big difference in our ability to persist during a long study session, especially because these needs tend to be fairly nagging if unattended to.

Finally, it is essential to understand that, while we may feel that we are well poised to avoid and overcome these distractions, research has clearly shown that successfully avoiding distractions, like those listed above, actually takes a lot of energy.[2] We only have a limited supply of energy available to us (in the form of blood glucose) and, as we use it up by overcoming distractions, we are less and less able to avoid giving in. This epic battle between our ability to self-regulate and our desire to give in to distractions constantly rages on. As we subject ourselves to more distractions, we are less able to persevere with good habits. Thus, ensuring that we are not exposed to such distractions in the first place (by choosing a good study space) can make a big difference in our ability to maintain good study habits.

DISCUSSION QUESTION

↠ Have you ever had a study session completely deteriorate as you give in to distractions?

ACTION ITEM

↠ Experiment with setting some ground rules for avoiding study session distractions.

FOLLOW-UP

↠ Post your ground rules on social media so your friends can help you stick to them.

Relocation

Frequently, once we have an established routine in life (such as an ineffective, yet comfortable study space), it is very difficult to break from this norm and approach the situation from a new angle. This is largely due to a neurological phenomenon that is best understood through the use of the metaphor of pathways in a forest. Through repeated use, neural pathways in our brain become highly established just like game trails in a forest, which are stabilized and endure through repeated use. When walking through a forest, traveling along these pathways is much easier than traipsing through the undergrowth. In fact, even if one decided to create a new pathway through the forest by taking a new route, it would take months, if not years, for the new pathway to become established and the old pathway to become overgrown. This is exactly how our neurological pathways work as well.

Anytime we have become used to a given strategy or approach to some aspect of our lives, changing that strategy, even after it stops being effective, can be extremely difficult. This is why addicts have such a hard time giving up their extremely destructive addictions. The tendency is to struggle against the change by returning to the old path, rather than creating and sticking to a new path. However, overcoming this struggle and resisting the urge to return to our old habits is imperative if we want to achieve real success, especially in the realm of study habits.

One common occurrence is for a person to find a study space that is initially very productive and which provides the needed relief from distractions. However, it is not uncommon for such productive spaces to become polluted over time with influences and habits that are not conducive to studying. Once this happens, relocation becomes highly desirable, although, just like creating new paths in a forest, somewhat challenging. Remembering how critical distraction-free study environments can be to successful study habits can give encouragement to individuals to make this change.

Additionally, due to the difficulty of finding productive study spaces in the first place, it's always better to protect productive study spaces from becoming polluted, rather than having to resort to relocation. Good habits are far easier to defend when maintained, rather than to reform once they are broken.

DISCUSSION QUESTION

⮑ Have any of your favorite study spaces ever become polluted by distractions?

ACTION ITEM

⮑ If your current study space is ineffective, scout out one possible alternative.

FOLLOW-UP

⮑ Report your findings in an email to a helping-professional you like and trust.

Productive Ambiance

Have you ever thought about how little details about a room, like how comfortable your chair is, what the room temperature is, the color of the paint, or how well lit the space is, have a direct impact on how long and how efficiently you are able to study?

Research done by the Swiss Federal Institute of Technology has shown that individuals who are exposed to artificial light during the afternoon, rather than natural light, are significantly sleepier during the evening.[3] In other words, if a student spends the afternoon in artificial light and then attempts to have an evening study session, they may quickly find themselves very tired. In contrast, an individual who spends the afternoon in natural light is far more likely to feel refreshed in the evening and able to conduct a productive study session. The lighting of a study space can also affect your ability to focus by being too bright or too dim, both of which can result in eye strain.

A study conducted by Cornell University found that temperature has a significant effect on your ability to study effectively and make fewer mistakes. Dr. Alan Hedge found that, by simply raising the temperature from 68 degrees to 77 degrees, research participants not only reduced their typing errors by 44%, but also increased their typing speed by 150%.[4] Over time, the savings of working in a nicely temperate environment add up to a huge difference in an individual's overall performance.

In another area of research, aromatherapy, Dr. Mark Moss of Northumbria University found that being exposed to the essential oil Rosemary improved the memory of participants by 60-75%.[5] This finding was supported by other research that has shown that Rosemary oil also increases alertness. Who knew that something as simple as scent could have such a profound impact on memory?

Finally, author Faber Birren, in his book "The Power of Color," presented research that showed that colorful walls, as opposed to white or off white, increased efficiency by as much as 28%.[6] All of this remarkable research points to the important reality that locating a colorful study environment, in addition to one that is well-lit and nicely temperate and possibly aesthetically aromatic, can easily mean the difference between earning an A or a B on the test you're studying for.

DISCUSSION QUESTION

❧ Describe your current study location. Is it well lit? Nicely colorful? Warm enough?

ACTION ITEM

❧ Experiment with changing the lighting or temperature of your study space.

FOLLOW-UP

❧ Post your findings on social media and discuss your results with a helping-professional.

Music & Mood

Many people have heard about how certain music, for example the music for Mozart and Bach, is supposed to make you smarter and help you study. While this phenomenon is technically true (and not nearly as straightforward as that), it's actually happening for reasons different than most people think. The reality is that the music is actually acting as a mood enhancer, elevating the listener's emotional state and causing them to experience advantageous side effects of something called mild positive affect [happy feelings], which tend to improve creative problem solving (see page 59 for more information about this phenomenon). As researchers who study this effect have pointed out, "Systematic changes made in tempo (fast vs. slow) and in mode (happy vs. sad) [within pieces of music] have significant effects on mood,"[7] which is exactly what causes the listener to feel happier and perform more efficiently on their homework.

To add another layer to this fascinating area of research, it's important to understand that there isn't even anything particularly special about the music of Mozart or Bach, because similar results have been found for much simpler music, including even children's songs. These results are due to the fact that, more than any other kind of music, the music that the listener likes most and which makes them feel good tends to be exactly the kind of music that they should listen to while studying. The idea that people benefit most from music that they actually like is called the Iso Principle, and it is something that music psychologists have been trying to popularize amongst the general population for years.

While the music that is going to be most beneficial to any study session is the music that the listener likes the best, does that mean that the listener can choose any kind of music and achieve the same kind of results?

Sadly, the answer is no. Music that is particularly jarring, loud, or that includes yelling, profanity, or particularly suggestive lyrics actually tends to be fairly distracting, even if it is something that the listener likes. Interestingly, the brain is actually easily distracted by loud, jarring noises and attends more intensely to profanity and suggestive language than it does to words like house, dog, car, and tree. For this reason, music that does not contain any lyrics at all (instrumental) tends to be a safe choice for any given study session, especially music that the listener likes and responds well to in terms of mood.

DISCUSSION QUESTION

    ❧ What kinds of music do you like to listen to?

ACTION ITEM

    ❧ Try listening to this music during your next study session.

FOLLOW-UP

    ❧ Report your findings by email to a helping-professional or using social media.

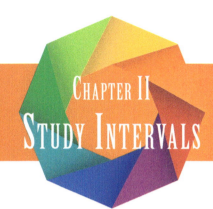

Chapter II
Study Intervals

Take a Break

A wide body of research has shown the benefits of taking regular breaks during study sessions. While many different lengths of time have been suggested, 10 minutes out of every hour is a reasonable expectation. Some individuals prefer two five minute breaks, each after 25 minutes, while others prefer one 10 minute break at the end of 50 minutes. Regardless of which you prefer, know that taking a break from your work is essential to maintaining productive study habits.

Good study breaks have the following characteristics:

1. In order to get your blood flowing again and feeding your mind the required oxygen, stand up and walk around during each break: go to the bathroom, get a drink, or take a lap around the building to get some fresh air.

2. Always engage in a different kind of activity while taking a study break. If you have been reading a lot while studying, don't take a break by reading a magazine. If you have been working at a computer, don't take a break by checking social media.

3. Refuel your mind. Eating a healthy snack or drinking some water can make a big difference in how productive you are during a study session.

Finally, do not be afraid to take a long break from studying. Research has shown that longer study breaks lead to the best retention over time. One study concluded that "learning at one single point in time impaired learning, compared with a several-minute interval between study episodes" resulting in up to a 15% benefit during assessment.[1] In other words, longer breaks are not only easier to take, but they actually help us perform better during tests.

DISCUSSION QUESTION

    ⊺ Have you noticed yourself feeling drained during study sessions that don't include breaks?

ACTION ITEM

    ⊺ During your next 3 study sessions, take a break that involves walking and a drink of water.

FOLLOW-UP

    ⊺ Post the results of your experiment on social media or share with a helping-professional.

Review Often

The widespread occurrence of procrastination has led some students to believe that cramming sessions are not only valuable, but a normal or even preferred method of study. Research has not only shown this not to be true, but has established a clear record of the success of reviewing class material early and at frequent intervals.

In fact, earlier and more frequent studying not only correlates with success on assessments, but also shows a strong impact on retention of the material many months later. For courses in a student's major and for subjects that build on past material over time, reviewing often is critical to success in the course. Researchers at Lancaster University concluded that "separating learning episodes by a period of at least one day, rather than concentrating all learning into one session, is extremely useful for maximizing long-term retention."[2] In fact, distributed practice was found by researchers at Kent State University to be one of the most effect study skills of those evaluated within their study.[3]

Another study showed that our minds actually continue to attempt to solve particularly difficult problems during periods of sleep: "After a period of sleep, wake, or no delay, participants reattempted previously unsolved problems. The sleep group solved a greater number of difficult problems than did the other groups."[4] This means that breaking up study sessions to occur on different days can actually save us time by allowing our minds to continue to work through the problem as we sleep.

In conclusion, ensuring that you have blocked off time throughout your week to dedicate to reviewing difficult material is essential to your overall success in the course. Daily review of the material is perhaps the most important and effective way to ensure that you are studying at appropriate intervals.

DISCUSSION QUESTION

↝ Have you seen any added benefit from reviewing material early and often?

ACTION ITEM

↝ Break up a single hour study session that you've planned into three 20 minute sessions.

FOLLOW-UP

↝ Report the findings of your experiment to a helping-professional you like and trust.

"Personal Time Survey"

George Mason University developed the following formula[5] to help students examine their weekly schedule. Fill in the information to determine how much time you are allowing yourself to study each week:

1. "Hours slept each night   _____ X 7 = _____

2. "Hours spent grooming each day   _____ X 7 = _____

3. "Hours spent preparing and enjoying meals each day   _____ X 7 = _____

4. "Weekday travel time   _____ X 5= _____

5. "Weekend travel time   _____

6. "Hours spent each week participating in regularly occurring events such as church or other meetings   _____

7. "Hours spent on daily chores   _____ X 7 = _____

8. "Hours of work each week   _____

9. "Hours spent in class each week (usually equal to number of credits)   _____

10. "Hours, on average, spent socializing each week   _____

11. "Add up the far right column of numbers here   _____

12. "Subtract this sum from 168   168 - _____ = _____

"The remaining hours are the amount of time you have allowed yourself to study each week."[5]

After taking this survey, many students find that they have an abundance of free time (40+ hours) that they can't account for. This is usually due to the fact that we rarely have huge chunks of free time, but tend to have lots of 10-20 minute periods of time that add up. Using these 10-20 minute time periods to study can be an especially effective way of reviewing course material on a frequent basis, rather than just passing the time.

DISCUSSION QUESTION

  ❧ Do you think you could study during 20 minute breaks that you have throughout the day?

ACTION ITEM

  ❧ Identify one area in your schedule where you waste time. Commit to improving this area.

FOLLOW-UP

  ❧ Report your commitment on social media and ask your friends to help you succeed.

Engram Maintenance

Everyone experiences the process of remembering past events, but few stop to think about what memory actually looks like in real life, deep inside our brains. Books like *Harry Potter*, for example, have given us a very believable fiction that memories look like little wispy clouds containing visual information that fades in and out like a fuzzy monitor. The actual substance of memories is something that has evaded scientists for a very long time. More than a hundred years ago, an influential scientist named Richard Semon theorized that memories must exist in physical space and, while he wasn't quite sure where in the brain this was or what memory looked like, he decided to give the physical substance of memories a name: engrams.[6]

While engrams have been theorized to exist for a very long time, it wasn't until recently that they were actually discovered: individual neurons are coded with our memories through an electrochemical process that still isn't fully understood.[7] Nonetheless, one thing that is understood quite well is the fact that whether or not memories are long lasting is entirely dependent on a number of very important factors. These variables include how strongly the information was originally coded (for example, particularly emotional memories have a better chance of being recalled), how thoroughly and intricately connected those memories are to other information stored in our brains, and how frequently the information is used.

As for how frequently our memories are used, reviewing material often is a critical aspect of strengthening our memories through *engram maintenance*. The number of times we have reviewed a specific memory or piece of information is directly related to how familiar with that information we will be. Familiarity is entirely a function of consistent and recurrent exposure to the same information, which is exactly why the word *family*, something to which we are regularly exposed, is a direct reference to the word *familiar*.

As an example of how one might review class material more often, a student named Curtis was known for recording class lectures, editing the recordings at home to exclude all of the long pauses and nonsense, and then listening to the edited recordings (which were now about half as long as the full class) at 3 times speed on the bus ride to school the following day. In this way, he was able to listen to one lecture 4-5 times before hearing any new material. This type of engram maintenance is not only highly sophisticated, but a great way to instill a sense of confidence in the material.

DISCUSSION QUESTION

↝ Can you think of anything to make frequent review sessions more efficient or less boring?

ACTION ITEM

↝ Review the same material five times on one day and then check your memory a week later.

FOLLOW-UP

↝ Report your findings in an email to a helping-professional or on social media after a test.

Tracking Progress

One astounding principle of psychology and, subsequently, behavioral modification is the principle that simply studying something changes it. This is called the Hawthorne Effect and, if you're willing, you can use it to improve your general well-being. The term was coined in 1950 by an experimenter named Henry Landsberger who had performed a study in the Hawthorne electric factory in Illinois. The productivity of the factory workers improved drastically simply because and for no other reason than the fact that they realized they were being studied.[8]

What's surprising is that, relying on the Hawthorne Effect, you can select any given target behavior (overeating, poor sleep habits, bad posture), keep a record of that behavior, and the behavior will naturally begin to change—hopefully for the better! Perhaps a person is aware that, over the past few months, they have been gaining weight. Futile attempts to casually reduce their portions has left this person feeling like weight-gain is an inevitable part of life. So, harnessing the power of the Hawthorne Effect, this person simply begins to keep a food diary; they track when they eat, how much they eat, how many times a day they eat, how they felt before and after eating, and how their weight changes day by day. Subsequently, the individual naturally and intuitively begins to draw fairly accurate conclusions about the behaviors that precipitate the weight gain, simply because they have access to a long-term record of the behavior and can now see patterns in that behavior.

Human beings are hard-wired to detect patterns and to draw conclusions from the patterns that they detect. When presented with ambiguous stimuli, human beings will immediately begin to impose structure onto that ambiguity. Because of this natural inclination, the elements of the target behavior that previously seemed illusive begin to reveal themselves through a well-kept record. Maybe we keep a food diary and then realize we eat when we're sleepy or when we're bored. Maybe we suddenly deduce, because we've started to keep a sleep diary that our most restless nights occur on days that we forget to exercise.

These same principles can also be used to track aspects of our academic well-being and hopefully help us work to improve study habits and attitudes we have towards school. For example, students can choose to track the time of day or location that they complete their homework along with the grades they receive for the work. Similarly, they can track the number of hours they spend studying for an exam compared to how confident they feel on the morning of the test and their relative performance compared to other test days. All of these variables, when properly tracked, worked together to provide a clear picture of what is working for the student and what needs to be changed.

DISCUSSION QUESTION

↝ What kind of academic behaviors do you think could be tracked in this way?

ACTION ITEM

↝ Keep a record of the amount of time you spend studying before each of three tests.

FOLLOW-UP

↝ Share your test scores and hours spent studying with a helping-professional or friend.

Course Attendance

A common occurrence amongst college students is a failure to attend class on a consistent and regular basis. Many reasons are used to justify instances of poor attendance, but few are ultimately legitimate when viewed in the larger scheme of academic well-being. Barring illness and emergency, there are almost no "good excuses" for missing class.

A major influencing factor that contributes to the tendency to miss class amongst college students is the fact that attendance in high school is not only expected but is an obligation imposed on the student by the school and, usually, by parents. Once a student reaches the university level, however, no such expectation is held by the institution (at least not actively) and there is rarely someone on hand, like a parent, to ensure that the student rolls out of bed and makes it to class on time.

While many college students enjoy this new found dynamic of personal freedom, few stop to realize that missing class is not only foolish in most cases, but a terrible waste of money. Tuition costs for one class at a typical four-year public institution when broken down can be as much as $20-30 per one hour lecture. This sunk cost is something that the student has already paid and which will never be refunded. Unfortunately, many college students do not stop to realize that this is the first time in their entire lives that they are actually paying more for a service and, through their own actions, getting less. This is similar to placing and paying for an order at a drive-thru and then failing to pick it up at the window.

In addition to the financial considerations, missing class has the added consequence of creating a rift in the continuity of the course. Most subjects, especially math and sciences, have material that builds directly on previously presented concepts. As such, missing one day of class might have exponential consequences as students race to catch up on the material. In fact, research has shown that consistent class attendance can result in an improvement in tests scores by as much as 7.7%.[9] Few students, if any, can afford to leave such valuable percentage points on the table.

DISCUSSION QUESTION

    ❧ For what reasons do you find yourself wanting to miss class?

ACTION ITEM

    ❧ Next time you want to skip class, go. Afterwards, write 3 good things that occurred in class.

FOLLOW-UP

    ❧ Report your experience on social media or through an email to a helping-professional.

Homework and Reading

Procrastination is a common epidemic on college campuses, where students feel that they can save up all of their homework and reading until the night before it is due or the night before the test. While homework and text book reading can often feel like busy work, it is beneficial to remember that the more exposure one has to a subject, the more proficiency will be developed. It's also important to understand that exposure to the material isn't just about the total number of hours spent studying, but also about the number of instances of exposure across multiple days.

Research has clearly shown that cram sessions are not as effective as spreading the material out across several days and study sessions. Taking the time to review class material and to read the text book on a daily basis may seem very difficult, but amazingly might end up taking less time than doing a cram session. As students get used to spending relatively shorter periods of time each day working on course material (rather than attempting all their studying during one long cram session), they will realize that study sessions have to be neither painful nor drawn out in order to be effective.

Completing homework and readings *well* before the last minute also allows the student to employ their inquiry skills to further investigate material that isn't entirely understood. Saving this work until the night before an exam, for example, usually results in sloppy outcomes, simply because there isn't enough time to finish everything and go the extra mile to understand those especially difficult concepts. Additionally, studying at night tends to be more stressful, simply because our cortisol levels, which help us to cope with stress and have more accurate memory, are significantly lower at night than in the morning·

Just like exercising the body, the mind benefits from short repetitions of the same material, rather than one long session of tiring study. Plan to set aside time every day to work on your most difficult courses. Again shorter periods of study each and every day can be more than enough when compared to cram sessions, as long as this behavior continues throughout the week and at regular intervals.

DISCUSSION QUESTION

→ Why do you think students have a tendency to put off their work until the last minute?

ACTION ITEM

→ Spread your work across multiple days and then reflect on its impact on your success.

FOLLOW-UP

→ Report your experiences to a helping-professional you like and trust.

Seek Resources Early and Often

At some point or another on their course to graduation, many students realize that they need more assistance in their academic lives than they previously supposed. Sometimes this means getting a tutor or attending a study group. Other times, students need to seek help from an academic advisor or professional counselor. Whatever the case may be, students, who tend to be fairly busy, often put off seeking out resources for another day, with the expectation that the services will always be available.

Unfortunately, once this search has been put off for another day, many students fail to finally carry through and make the appointment or finally walk through the door to speak with a program representative. Since almost all resources available on a college campus are free, students do themselves a disservice by wasting the opportunity to get the help early, when research has shown it has the most impact.

For example, students who seek tutoring early (within the first 2 weeks of the quarter or semester) not only have a much more productive experience, but also spend more time working with the tutor throughout the span of the course, resulting in a better understanding of the material right from the start. Conversely, students that seek tutoring after their course is already half-way over tend to have comparatively dismal results.

Of course, the ability of resources that are offered on campus to help students be successful is entirely dependent on students making themselves available, early and often, to participate in those services.

DISCUSSION QUESTION

    ‣ What resource do you wish you had known about or used earlier in your college career?

ACTION ITEM

    ‣ Find a previously unused resource in Chapter 7 and check-it out.

FOLLOW-UP

    ‣ Post your findings on social media or share them with a helping-professional you trust.

CHAPTER III
STUDY METHOD

Individual Differences

Many students have favorite study methods that they're accustomed to using but may not have tried any other strategies, simply because they may not know what other methods are available to them. This is likely due to the fact that study habits are more often "picked up" rather than learned from doing research or in a formal setting. Learning about how to learn is usually something only education majors spend a lot of time on. Due to this aspect of study skills development, many students maintain habits that may be convenient, but may not be particularly successful. Researchers at Kent State University even demonstrated that some of the most popular study methods, such as highlighting texts, rereading, and summarization are some of the most ineffective strategies.[1] In light of these realities, students may not know how to change their study habits or, even if they want to, how to go about it effectively.

In order to develop better study habits, students have to be willing to do some informal research. A great way to do this is simply by asking friends and classmates about their favorite study methods and tricks. Based on the given responses, the student can then try each new method on for size to see how it works out. Keeping in mind that what works for one person does not necessarily work for everyone, students should not become discouraged if certain methods don't happen to pan out for them. Instead, students should try out as many as they can until they find a method that works well for them.

Finding just the right study method might take a few weeks or even a few months. Students may also find that what works for one subject, may not work for another and so on. During the entire process of seeking out new methods of studying, students should be encouraged to be flexible. Willingness to learn new things is a critical aspect of acquiring and effectively implementing new study skills.

DISCUSSION QUESTION

- How do you think your friends would react to you asking about their study methods?

ACTION ITEM

- Approach one friend or classmate about their favorite study methods and try one out.

FOLLOW-UP

- Report the experience in an email to a helping-professional you like or trust.

Multiple Intelligences

Research has shown that IQ (Intelligence Quotient) is not actually that a great of an indicator of overall life success. People who have higher IQs do not necessarily make more money, have higher educational attainment, or report higher quality of life. Due to this reality, Howard Gardner, an Educational Psychologist at Harvard University, theorized that Multiple Intelligences exist in each and every one of us and that these intelligences are the building blocks of our true potential. Eight of the Multiple Intelligences that Gardner first identified appear below.[2]

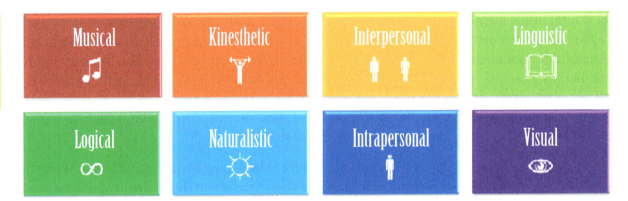

Each individual has their own unique combination of all eight intelligences, giving each one of us remarkable strengths and value. When viewed through this lens of intellectual diversity, everyone becomes smart *in their own way*. Recognizing individual strengths allows us to see success as a multi-facetted opportunity available to everyone, according to their strengths and interests rather than a one-size-fits-all standard of achievement. As Albert Einstein once said, "Everybody is a genius. But if you judge a fish by its ability to climb a tree, it will live its whole life believing that it is stupid."

To discover an individual's Multiple Intelligences, access the associated questionnaire available on the resources page of *www.studysimpler.com* or acquire a copy of Dr. Thomas Armstrong's book, *Multiple Intelligences in the Classroom*.[3]

DISCUSSION QUESTION

➤ How does knowing about Multiple Intelligences help you orient yourself to your studies?

ACTION ITEM

➤ Locate and take the MI survey to discover your personal Multiple Intelligences.

FOLLOW-UP

➤ Schedule a discussion about the results of your test with a helping-professional you trust.

Bloom's Taxonomy

In 1956, Benjamin Bloom outlined a taxonomy of learning objectives[4] that emphasizes the importance of engaging coursework with as much inquiry and depth as possible. At the base of his taxonomy, we find the most rudimentary form of knowledge—simply Remembering. As we move up the taxonomy, the depth of processing advances and the likelihood that the information will be recalled during assessment increases in measure. Using the diagram below, begin to explore the organization of the taxonomy and the various stages of engagement that students can use to master material:

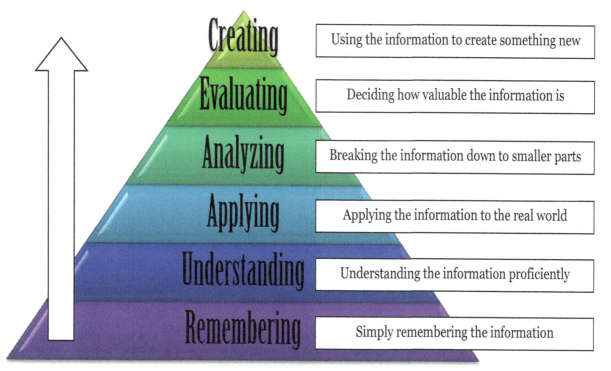

Creating	Using the information to create something new
Evaluating	Deciding how valuable the information is
Analyzing	Breaking the information down to smaller parts
Applying	Applying the information to the real world
Understanding	Understanding the information proficiently
Remembering	Simply remembering the information

As we work on course material, it is imperative to ensure that we are always striving to work up the taxonomy towards the highest level of curricular attainment, using the information in ever more complex ways. Sadly, most instruction and study strategies only engage the learner at the lowest two levels of the taxonomy, which emphasizes the importance of taking personal responsibility to move up the pyramid for oneself during personal study sessions.

DISCUSSION QUESTION

   ❧ What step of the pyramid do you find you spend most of your time and energy on?

ACTION ITEM

   ❧ During your next study session, select one of the top three levels to experiment with.

FOLLOW-UP

   ❧ Share your experiences with classmates or with a helping-professional you like and trust.

Notetaking Skills

There are many different ways to take notes in class, but not all methods are created equal. Our minds process information from a standpoint of identifying unique qualities that distinguish certain types of information from other types. Visual and spatial information are particularly memorable and can help us take better notes. For example, you may have had the experience of remembering where something was in a book not by the page number, but by where it was located on the page. Similarly, when driving to a familiar location, you might remember how to get there not by street names and distances but by landmarks along the way. In this same manner, giving our mind *visual* landmarks in our notes helps us remember the information.

Here are some helpful tips to including more visually memorable landmarks on your notes pages:

1. Using different hand written font styles for different sections of the material (all-caps, cursive, print, bold, italics, underline, larger, smaller) can help our memories to visually separate pieces of information that we've written down.

2. Avoiding taking notes on a laptop or in an environment where all of the text is identical to all of the other text can also help.

3. Using stars and other symbols in the margins of notes to indicate information that will likely to be on the test is critical to deciding what to study.

4. Using different colors of ink on different days can help, too. This is different than switching different colors of ink during the same lecture, which can be distracting.

5. Highlighting certain information as we review the notes can be helpful. However, remember this simple truth: if everything is highlighted, then nothing is. In fact, researchers from Kent State University recently demonstrated that highlighting/underlining textbooks is actually one of the least effective study techniques of those evaluated in their study.[5]

As students begin to experiment with visually stimulating styles of notetaking their ability to engage the classroom material and remember the concepts more proficiently will develop in a very tangible way. The key is to ensure that all of the notes are being coded in a visually differentiated manner.

DISCUSSION QUESTION

    ❧ Are you satisfied with your current notetaking strategies? Could they improve?

ACTION ITEM

    ❧ Experiment with visually stimulating styles of notetaking throughout the following week.

FOLLOW-UP

    ❧ Compare your notes with a classmate or ask a helping-professional to assess your efforts.

Managing Test Anxiety

Test anxiety is an extremely common phenomenon that has many causes, which differ from one student to the next. Due to the many different kinds of text anxiety that occur, there is no one 'magic bullet' that can help everyone manage test anxiety, although there are a lot of helpful tips that might do the trick.

Mark Gilbert and Karen Gilbert, two educators from British Columbia, recognizing the vast array of information available about this topic, assembled a 17-page packet of materials from multiple sources that can be used to effectively engage this topic.[6]

The packet, which is available online (linked on the resources page of *www.studysimpler.com*), has many helpful tips, questions and exercises that individuals can work through over the course of several days or even several weeks to better understand their own anxiety and seek possible solutions.

DISCUSSION QUESTION	
↬ Have you ever experienced test anxiety and had it negatively impact your performance?	
ACTION ITEM	
↬ Work through the Test Anxiety packet and identify your favorite section.	
FOLLOW-UP	
↬ Share your favorite section of the packet with friends through email or on social media.	

Active Listening

Nationally recognized public speaker Russ Peterson explains, "The average speaker speaks at about 125 words per minute, [while] the average listener can comprehend about four times higher —500 words per minute!" This means that "if you have one person sitting right up front [in your mind] listening… you've got three in back getting bored."[7]

The nature of these ratios emphasizes the importance of listening more actively and engaging more of our mind during the process of learning, especially within a lecture setting. One way to approach this is to think of something for each of those three extra "people" in your mind to do while the fourth attends to the straightforward task of listening. Interestingly, the Chinese character for Listen is actually made up of four different symbols, which emphasize the many aspects of active listening.

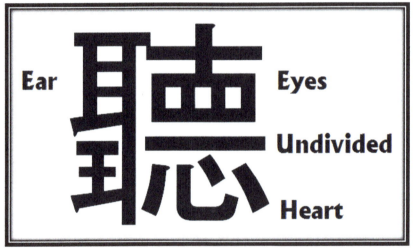

Perhaps one way to more fully engage our minds in the process of listening is to remember to listen with our eyes and hearts, as well as with our ears. What do we see in the room that helps us understand the information more fully? What about the speaker's presentation? Does their style connect with us emotionally or with our past experiences? Answering these questions can help us engage course material as active listeners that use more than just the ears as a tool for listening.

DISCUSSION QUESTION

➤ What are some things that you have found that make it difficult to listen during class?

ACTION ITEM

➤ Make a copy of the character pictured above and tape it to the front of your notebook.

FOLLOW-UP

➤ Share this information with friends or classmates using social media. Note their reaction.

Organizational Skills

One of the most unusual and persistent myths about organization is that good organization is a sign that individuals have their act together. In reality, almost everyone has some system of organization that works well for them, although some people's methods are more uniform and orderly than others. For example, many creative researchers have stacks and stacks of books and papers piled all over their office. In fact, there is a well-known picture of former Vice-President Al Gore, sitting in his home office in front of several large computer monitors, surrounded by mountains of books and papers. People like Al Gore might seem messy, but they tend to know exactly where everything is because they're the ones that put it there. In fact, if a well-meaning friend or relative were to attempt to straighten their piles and stacks, the person may very well not be able to find a single thing afterwards. Dr. Steven Reiss of the Ohio State University explains in his book, *The Normal Personality*, that this exact kind of incident occurred between him and his wife Maggi, who happens to be a more uniformly organized person than he is. She thought that she was helping her messy husband tidy up a bit, when, in reality, she was messing up his disorderly organization.[8]

Organizational methods are about individual style. What works for one person may not work for another. However, regardless of one's current system of organization, it is extremely helpful to constantly be on the lookout for systems of organization that might improve one's current functioning. Asking friends or more knowledgeable peers about their styles of organization can be extremely interesting and helpful. After experimenting, you may find that their systems work well for you or not. Either way, being open and flexible to better organization habits is crucial to academic success and is something that can only be developed over time and through personal experience.

DISCUSSION QUESTION

    ❧ There are many different styles of organization; how would you describe your style?

ACTION ITEM

    ❧ Approach one friend or classmate about their favorite organization tricks and try one out.

FOLLOW-UP

    ❧ Take pictures of your efforts and share them on social media to solicit encouragement.

Fluency and Speed

There are two aspects of knowledge that professors are able measure in order to assess student proficiency with course material: Fluency, which is the degree to which the student understands the material, and Speed, which is how quickly the student can produce that knowledge on an assessment. This means that all students can be classified into one of three domains of proficiency:

1. Low Speed / Low Fluency: Taking a long time to achieve incorrect answers

2. Low Speed / High Fluency: Taking a long time to achieve correct answers

3. High Speed / High Fluency: Taking a short time to achieve correct answers

There is also technically a fourth domain (High Speed / Low Fluency), but nobody is impressed by someone who gets the wrong answer quickly.

In most situations, students work to achieve understanding of the material first, rather than focusing on speed. This initial step from Low Fluency to High Fluency, while maintaining Low Speed, is an arduous process that can be very frustrating. Interestingly, the difficulty of transitioning from Low Fluency to High Fluency also creates a hidden pitfall. Frequently, the moment at which a student transitions from Low Fluency to High Fluency (step 1 to step 2 above) is a very exciting one! Students become very thrilled by this "Aha!" moment and often throw a miniature celebration of success. Unfortunately, this milestone usually prompts students to quickly transition to newer material, since High Fluency has already been achieved with the previous section.

This instinct is misleading since the transition into High Fluency has only moved the student from the 1st domain into the 2nd, while their speed has remained low. Unfortunately, the student has yet to transition into the 3rd and most proficient domain: High Fluency *and* High Speed. Unless this final step is made, students' test grades tend to be much lower than their homework grades.

Students should feel encouraged to celebrate upon arriving in the second domain, but should not allow this celebration to prevent them from continuing to put forth effort in transitioning into the third domain through timed practice problems, sample quizzes, and practice tests. All of these tools can make a big difference between a student who merely understands the material and one who is able to demonstrate their understanding quickly during a test. In fact, researchers at Kent State University found that timed preactice is one of the most effective study techniques students can use.[9]

DISCUSSION QUESTION

→ Have you ever felt prepared for a test only to find out that you've run out of time taking it?

ACTION ITEM

→ In preparation for your next test, create and work through one or two time practice tests.

FOLLOW-UP

→ After receiving your scores, schedule a discussion with a helping-professional you trust.

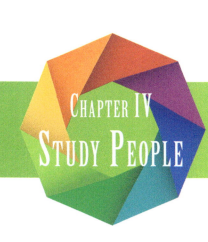

CHAPTER IV
STUDY PEOPLE

Introversion vs. Extraversion

Carl Jung, a 20th century psychologist, theorized that two main attitudes to life are integral components of understanding an individual's personality. One attitude, Introversion, primarily involves a private, less social world of reflection and contemplation, while the other attitude, Extraversion, involves a highly social, activity-oriented style of life. Because the two styles are so different from each other, misunderstandings between individuals who possess different styles can occur easily.

As far as Introversion and Extraversion relate to study habits, each attitude presents its own set of assets and liabilities to academic success:

Individuals who are more Introverted tend to prefer to study individually or with a single partner and can be extremely productive in their study habits when compared to individuals who are more extraverted. Introverts can study for long periods of time without experiencing the need for a social break and are known for their ability to immerse themselves in books. As a result of these habits, Introverts tend to have higher GPAs than Extraverts and they are also more likely to be found studying on a Friday night.[1]

Extraverts derive their energy from interactions they have with other people. They are more likely to study with large groups of classmates and seek more casual settings for their study sessions, such as couches and beds.[1] While they benefit from exchanging ideas with others, their sociable nature can also lead to a lot of non-academic discussion during study sessions. Extraverts should feel encouraged to study with peers, as an incentive for getting the work done, but should also avoid studying with people they are especially social with. Maintaining such boundaries with classmates, while still gleaning the benefits of group study, can be crucial to academic success.

To determine your personality style, access the resources page of *www.studysimpler.com*.

DISCUSSION QUESTION

↬ How does your social style effect the way you study?

ACTION ITEM

↬ Locate the free personality test linked on *www.studysimpler.com* to discover your type.

FOLLOW-UP

↬ Schedule a discussion to share you test results with a helping-professional you trust.

Social Influence

Whenever we develop a habit or way of doing things that is consistent over time, changing that behavior can be very difficult (for more discussion on this topic, see page 25). For this reason, when attempting to study with friends, we may find it difficult to avoid engaging in the kind of informal social interactions that are so common in every other area of our lives.

Humans, especially extraverts (see previous page), are hard-wired to not only be aware of their social surroundings but to have positive social interactions with those around them as well. For example, while we have many different types of memory, one entire section of our temporal lobe is dedicated specifically to remembering faces of people we have met before and nothing else. In fact, if this area becomes damaged, a surreal disorder called prosopagnosia develops, in which the individual loses all ability for facial recognition, including being unable to recognize members of their family, their spouse, and even themselves. This is just one physiological representation of just how important other people are to us and to our minds.

This social aspect of our nature means that we are especially susceptible to becoming distracted by social interactions while studying. As such, the same kind of cognitive interference that can occur by choosing inadequate study locations (see *Study Space*, pages 23-25) can occur by choosing to study in environments that are too socially interactive or socially distracting. Perhaps the worst of all such distractions is having far too easy access to social media.

At the same time, while people can be one of the biggest distractions to productive study habits, being around other individuals with positive study habits can be just as beneficial. As a result of these conflicting dynamics of the way the social interactions influence study habits, you may choose to balance your social study habits by studying with individuals whom you do not otherwise spend time with outside of academic environments. This aids in the self-regulation process, since slipping into casual social conversation will not be as habitual with this more formal type of study partner.

DISCUSSION QUESTION

 ❧ To what extent have other people been a help or a distraction to your study habits?

ACTION ITEM

 ❧ Rate your current study partners on a scale of 1-10 for how distracting they are to you.

FOLLOW-UP

 ❧ For partners with high scores, consider changing your approach to sharing study sessions.

Teach to Learn

A remarkable way of learning new material is through instruction. Many tutors report that they appreciate the opportunity to share their knowledge with other students because doing so forces them to regularly review, reinternalize, and rehearse material that they have covered before. While not everyone has the opportunity to be a tutor, anyone can attempt to find others who might be willing to act as a student during a teach-to-learn session. Classmates, friends, family members, and even children or stuffed animals can be willing participants in this process.

The phenomenon of learning from instruction may seem paradoxical, but actually is the result of a fairly straightforward mechanism involved in the process. First, attempting to explain information to another person involves a great deal of organizational thinking and usually requires quite a bit of preparation. The speaker has to determine how to sequence each unit of information so that the entire presentation makes sense to the listener. Often, this process not only occurs very intuitively, but results in a more full awareness within the person doing the teaching of the systematic nature of the knowledge being presented. Also, working towards the deadline of beginning to provide an explanation can give the presenter much needed motivation to review the material in an in-depth manner.

Another common occurrence during the process of instruction is feeling inspired to include a related piece of information or an example in an effort to provide a more interesting explanation to the listener. Acting on such inspirations allows the presenter to draw connections between meaningful sets of information, making the knowledge more salient and fully networked within their own mind.

Furthermore, during the process of instruction, the listener may ask questions that spark additional lines of investigation within the person presenting the material. Such questions, in addition to the unique nature of the listener and of the scenario (social memories are particularly powerful), help the instructor to have a vibrant mental record of the information and concepts presented in that instance of social interaction. These outcomes are not only rewarding during the process of recall, but also instill confidence in the presenter about their mastery of the material.

DISCUSSION QUESTION

 ❧ Have you ever tried to teach something to someone else in order to learn?

ACTION ITEM

 ❧ Identify one person who might be a good student for you to experiement on. Try it out.

FOLLOW-UP

 ❧ Share your experiences in a discussion with a helping-professional you like and trust.

Supplemental Instruction

Many institutions of higher education have programs that offer supplemental instruction for many of the most difficult courses on campus. The purpose of these study groups is to place a more knowledgeable peer as a facilitator amongst a small group of students (typically 8-15) from the course. These supplemental instruction groups are seldom meant to be lecture-style environments, but, rather, settings in which the facilitator and the students can collaborate and interact towards successful understanding of the material through active learning.

While such supplemental instruction groups would seem to be designed only for students who are struggling in the course, research shows that attendees include a nice mix of students from all academic levels, including many of the top students from the class. The collaborative nature of these environments means that all of the students in the group can benefit from each other's knowledge and recall of the material presented in class and in the text.

This type of active learning, which encourages group dynamics and group inquiry, is meant to provide students with a learning environment that highlights their ability to benefit from social interaction. This type of educational setting is not only interpersonally vibrant, but memorable and frequently fun.

To determine if your institution offers supplemental instruction groups, contact the student affairs or academic affairs division of your university or simply speak to your instructor about the availability of such resources. Research shows that students who regularly attend supplemental instruction groups score remarkably higher, on average, than classmates who do not.

DISCUSSION QUESTION

→ If you have attended a supplemental instruction group, what has been your experience?

ACTION ITEM

→ If your institution offers supplemental instruction groups, attend one at least five times.

FOLLOW-UP

→ Identify 3 good things you experienced in a thank-you email to the SI facilitator.

Get to Know Your Professors

Too often in the world of academia there is a culture of "Us vs. Them" when it comes to relations between students and professors. This terribly non-egalitarian approach to academic relationships is common amongst both students and professors and can be the cause of major problems and headaches for everyone involved.

On the whole, professors tend to be fantastic people to get to know and having a friendly relationship with them can have significant advantages. When dealing with a sea of students, many professors have trouble responding to requests for special consideration, since they may not know if any one particular student is truly responsible or just trying to slide by with an excuse. As such, developing a positive, open relationship with the professor, even in a very casual way, can mean the difference between receiving an understanding response to a special request or receiving a dismissive response for not being entirely on top of things.

An important aspect of fostering this type of positive relationship with professors is understanding how to approach and interact with professors in a positive way. Since professors tend to be fairly busy professionals, expecting that you can just speak to them immediately before or after class about important issues, when they may have many other things on their mind, can be terribly off-putting. Visit with professors during office hours, through email, or during other time periods when you know they are open to student interaction.

Additionally, it is important to understand that communicating with professors in a clear and concise way is something that they are likely to appreciate. Send emails that are short and to the point and that clearly identify yourself and the course you are in. Give them advance warning of class obligations that you know you are going to struggle fulfilling. Waiting until after a problem has already been created and then asking for help is a sign that you may not be as responsible as you'd like to appear. Furthermore, providing advanced and apologetic warning of absences (especially in smaller classes) can assuage the teacher into being lenient in helping you catch up on the material.

Just remember, most instructors remain employed in education because they ultimately enjoy helping students succeed. This means that they'll probably truly appreciate getting to know you as long as you are polite, considerate, and friendly in your interactions with them.

DISCUSSION QUESTION

↬ Do you tend to have fairly good relationships with your professors or not so much?

ACTION ITEM

↬ Make and keep one appointment with one professor you do not know very well.

FOLLOW-UP

↬ After the experience, report your experience on social media.

Building a Community of Support

Many students arrive to college feeling as though they are ready to take on the whole world and conquer university life like a super hero. Unfortunately, because college can be extremely challenging for many different reasons, the end of the first quarter or semester often leaves students feeling discouraged and unsure about the path ahead. Situations like a failing grade, a difficult breakup with a high school sweetheart, or a disappointing experience with a roommate can all leave students feeling deflated and hoping for much needed support.

Fortunately, no university expects their students to prevail against the rough tides of academia all by themselves. Universities offer a wide array of services that students should be ready and willing to access in order to overcome some of the most commonly experienced challenges and setbacks. Additionally, students should never underestimate the value of becoming involved in all of the student activities and services that are offered on campus. In fact, the reason that many universities offer a wide variety of social and extracurricular activities is because research has clearly shown that students who develop a good community within an institution are more likely to succeed.

As students sign up for clubs and orgs, attend university sponsored activities, and seek support through university resources, they will find themselves developing an ever more complex and supportive social web. This community of support will not only help the student to feel involved, but also give them a sense of belonging that is crucial to academic well-being. Such involvement in university programs and services has a direct impact on students' willingness to persist and graduate, especially in the face of opposition.

Students who are having a difficult time locating and accessing such services rarely have to look far for a more knowledgeable peer or a friendly staff member who would be willing to help them make the appropriate connections, especially with services resonate with the student's strengths and interests.

DISCUSSION QUESTION

➤ As a freshman, how did you locate and access services to help you succeed?

ACTION ITEM

➤ Identify one club or organization that you've been meaning to look into. Sign up!

FOLLOW-UP

➤ Share you experiences using social media, especially if you have a good time participating.

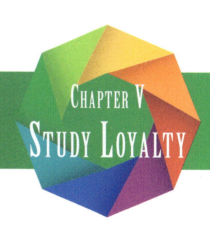

CHAPTER V
STUDY LOYALTY

Having a Positive Attitude

Attitude may not seem terribly relevant to how well you are doing in school, but research shows that how you are feeling strongly impacts your ability to function, think clearly, and even learn. In fact, having the right kind of positive attitude can make a big difference in how well you do in school and in everyday life. Research conducted by Alice M. Isen and her colleagues suggests that mild, positive feelings "induced in subtle, common ways"[1] lead to the following positive outcomes:

1. "Greater creativity

2. "Improved negotiation process and outcomes

3. "More thorough, open-minded, flexible thinking and problem solving

4. "Generosity & social responsibility

5. "Helpfulness

6. "Wanting to do what needs to be done

7. "More motivation to accomplish goals

8. "Greater openness to new information

9. "Thinking more clearly"[1]

These outcomes were most likely to occur in situations that were interesting or important to the person. These outcomes were also the result of happy feelings of the sort that most people experience every day (neither extreme nor unusual).[1]

DISCUSSION QUESTION

- What are some things in life that give you a good, positive feeling?

ACTION ITEM

- Before your next study session, watch a funny online video. See what effect it has on you.

FOLLOW-UP

- Share the results of your experiement using social media.

"The Hidden Power of Smiling"

Ron Gutman, the founder and CEO of HealthTap and graduate of Stanford University, offered a 7 ½ minute TED talk in 2011 called "The Hidden Power of Smiling."[2]

Watch his video on ted.com or youtube.com.

Some important points from Ron's talk:

1. "Success and well being throughout life can be predicted from measuring an individual's smile in their high school picture.

2. "The span of a smile can actually predict the span of a person's life.

3. "Smiling is contagious (smile + frown = smile).

4. "Mimicking another person's smile helps us figure out how they are feeling.

5. Facial Feedback Response Theory: "The act of smiling itself actually makes us feel better, rather than smiling merely being a result of feeling good.

6. "One smile can generate the same level of brain stimulation as up to 2,000 bars of chocolate… or $25,000 cash.

7. "Smiling reduces stress-inducing hormones, increases mood-enhancing hormones, and reduces overall blood pressure.

8. "Smiling makes you look good in the eyes of others; it makes you look more likable, courteous, and competent."[2]

DISCUSSION QUESTION

▸ How can this information change the way you approach studying?

ACTION ITEM

▸ Share the video with a friend or classmate. Watch them while it plays to see if they smile.

FOLLOW-UP

▸ Share your experiences on social media. Share the video, too, if you enjoyed watching it.

Victim vs. Creator

In his book "On Course: Strategies for Creating Success in College and in Life," Skip Downing outlines the difference between Victim Thinking and Creator Thinking.[3] This Responsibility Model is designed to help reflective students decide if their attitude toward their challenges in school has been effective or destructive to their overall well being. Victim Thinking usually causes the individual to engage in blaming of others (like the professor) or by blaming oneself or the circumstances, which leads to a sense of helplessness and low motivation. Creator Thinking, on the other hand, usually results in realizing that one's own efforts are primarily responsible for successes in life and that seeking solutions is the only way to change challenging setbacks into opportunities for success.

A clever story, written by Valerie Cox, illustrates this point quite well: "A woman was waiting at an airport one night, with several long hours before her flight. She hunted for a book in the airport shops, bought a bag of cookies and found a place to drop. She was engrossed in her book but happened to see, that the man sitting beside her, as bold as could be... grabbed a cookie or two from the bag in between, which she tried to ignore to avoid a scene. So she munched the cookies and watched the clock, as the gutsy cookie thief diminished her stock. She was getting more irritated as the minutes ticked by, thinking, 'If I wasn't so nice, I would blacken his eye.' With each cookie she took, he took one too, when only one was left, she wondered what he would do.

"With a smile on his face, and a nervous laugh, he took the last cookie and broke it in half. He offered her half, as he ate the other, she snatched it from him and thought... oooh, brother! This guy has some nerve and he's also rude, why he didn't even show any gratitude! She had never known when she had been so galled, and sighed with relief when her flight was called. She gathered her belongings and headed to the gate, refusing to look back at the thieving ingrate. She boarded the plane, and sank in her seat, then she sought her book, which was almost complete. As she reached in her baggage, she gasped with surprise, there was her bag of cookies, in front of her eyes. If mine are here, she moaned in despair, the others were his, and he tried to share. Too late to apologize, she realized with grief, that she was the rude one, the ingrate, the thief."[4]

The story is great because both characters actually find themselves in identical circumstances: both believe that the other person is eating their cookies. For the man, this happens to be reality, but he handles it with decorum and class. For the woman, who isn't quite in tune with reality, the situation becomes an opportunity for her to feel victimized. Why such a difference? Perhaps because the man understood how important it is to be a creator, even if things go terribly wrong.

DISCUSSION QUESTION
❧ Why is it so easy to engage in Victim Thinking instead of Creator Thinking?
ACTION ITEM
❧ Re-evaluate one area of your life where you have been taking a Victim stance.
FOLLOW-UP
❧ Schedule a discussion with a helping-professional to further explore these topics in depth.

Maslow's Hierarchy

Abraham Maslow, a significant 20th century psychological theorist, proposed the idea that each of us has a hierarchy of needs to which we are committed to fulfilling. Starting at the base of the hierarchy, with our most fundamental physiological needs like food, and continuing up to the top with the needs that give our life meaning, Maslow outlined the relative importance of each of our needs within this ascending hierarchy. Because our needs are organized in this manner, he explained, no one spends time worrying about their need to be creative if their need for food has not already been satisfied.[5]

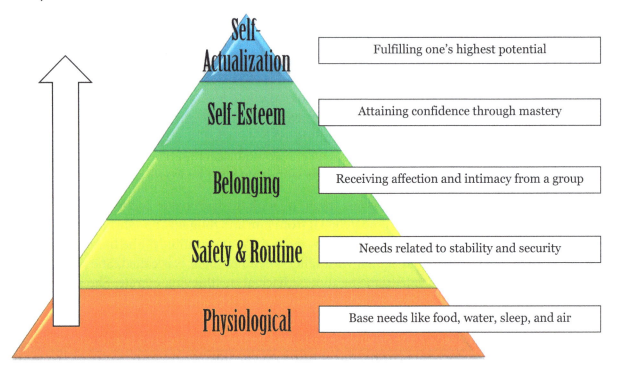

Interestingly, being truly motivated to learn for its own sake is a product of having regular and reliable access to the lowest four needs on the hierarchy: physiological needs, safety, belonging, and esteem. Once these are being regularly satisfied, an individual is free to pursue cognitive and aesthetic needs in a quest to become the best version of themselves, especially through academic pursuits.

DISCUSSION QUESTION

❦ Do you feel like your most basic needs are being met so you can focus on your education?

ACTION ITEM

❦ Journal about a time in your life when you felt your needs were being compromised.

FOLLOW-UP

❦ Be aware of your fellow students and look for opportunities to support anyone in need.

Atkinson's Model of Motivation

In 1956, psychologist John William Atkinson outlined the following formula[6] to help individuals think about what is truly motivating them to succeed:

Motivation (M) = Probability of Success (Ps) x Incentive of Success (Is)

The value of this formula is that it conceptualizes what many of us have experienced, but may not have been able to put into words. Basically, everyone is driven by a desire to succeed, but, as we all know, only when there is a good likelihood that we will succeed and be rewarded for that success. Without the likelihood for success or a good incentive for succeeding, many individuals will simply give up and move on to other rewarding pursuits, which provide them with a greater probability of achieving those rewards.

When an individual is considering the first part of the equation (their perception about how likely they are to succeed) the most important factor involved is their Self-Efficacy, which is discussed in greater depth on page 88 of this manual. While everyone has different levels of self-efficacy, the principle works roughly the same way for almost everyone. Those with higher self-efficacy are more likely to anticipate a higher probability of success than those with low self-efficacy.

In contrast, incentives for success work quite differently for everyone, since there are so many different ways that people can feel rewarded. A model for understanding these combinations of rewards, *The 16 Basic Desires*, is discussed in greater detail on the following page.

Students pursuing university level degrees have to be willing to consider both the probability of their success and the incentives for their success in all of their academic pursuits. Thankfully, there are ways to develop greater self-efficacy and also to more fully understand what drives each individual to succeed and how those incentives might be different for each of us.

DISCUSSION QUESTION

↜ What kind of things provide you with the greatest incentive in life? How about in school?

ACTION ITEM

↜ Journal about your goals for the future. Focus on incentives of achieving those successes.

FOLLOW-UP

↜ Share your journal entry during a visit with a helping-professional you trust and like.

Motivation Styles

Dr. Steven Reiss of the Ohio State University performed research that showed that all human motivation can be boiled down and explained through sixteen basic drives that everyone has, but which everyone experiences on different levels (weak strivings, average strivings, or strong strivings). In his book *Who am I?*, Dr. Reiss outlines these sixteen motivations and explains their importance in everyday life and relationships.[7]

Because everyone has a unique, personal motivation style, determining what motivates a student to be successful in school can be extremely helpful in figuring out what kind of encouragement can be used to help the student succeed. Each individual's combination of the sixteen motivations helps define their personality and explain why certain things are important to them, while other things are less important.

The following handout (available via the resources page of *www.studysimpler.com*) can be used to facilitate a discussion about how each student prioritizes the sixteen motivations in their own life.

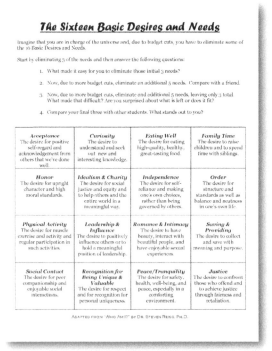

The Sixteen Basic Desires and Needs

Imagine that you are in charge of the universe and, due to budget cuts, you have to eliminate some of the 16 Basic Desires and Needs.

Start by eliminating 3 of the needs and then answer the following questions:

1. What made it easy for you to eliminate those initial 3 needs?
2. Now, due to more budget cuts, eliminate an additional 5 needs. Compare with a friend.
3. Now, due to more budget cuts, eliminate and additional 5 needs, leaving only 3 total. What made that difficult? Are you surprised about what is left or does it fit?
4. Compare your final three with other students. What stands out to you?

Acceptance The desire for positive self-regard and acknowledgement from others that we've done well.	**Curiosity** The desire to understand and seek out new and interesting knowledge.	**Eating Well** The desire for eating high-quality, healthy, great-tasting food.	**Family Time** The desire to raise children and to spend time with siblings.
Honor The desire for upright character and high moral standards.	**Idealism & Charity** The desire for social justice and equity and to help others and the entire world in a meaningful way.	**Independence** The desire for self-reliance and making one's own choices, rather than being governed by others.	**Order** The desire for structure and standards as well as balance and neatness in one's own life.
Physical Activity The desire for muscle exercise and activity and regular participation in such activities.	**Leadership & Influence** The desire to positively influence others or to hold a meaningful position of leadership.	**Romance & Intimacy** The desire to have beauty, interact with beautiful people, and have enjoyable sexual experiences.	**Saving & Providing** The desire to collect and save with meaning and purpose.
Social Contact The desire for peer companionship and enjoyable social interactions.	**Recognition for Being Unique & Valuable** The desire for respect and for recognition for personal uniqueness.	**Peace/Tranquility** The desire for safety, health, well-being, and peace, especially in a comforting environment.	**Justice** The desire to confront those who offend and to achieve justice through fairness and retaliation.

ADAPTED FROM "WHO AM I?" BY DR. STEVEN REISS, PH.D.

DISCUSSION QUESTION

↝ Work through the discussion questions provided on the handout.

ACTION ITEM

↝ Journal about how your results from the handout match specific goals you have in life.

FOLLOW-UP

↝ Share your three strongest and three weakest motivations with friends using social media.

Motivational Barriers

You may have a seen a popular diagram about how to deal with life's problems. For the sake of clarity, draw the diagram out as it is explained here. In the first square on the diagram, the question "Do you have a problem?" appears with arrows pointing to two answers: yes or no. If you follow the arrow through no, you're lead to a box that says "Then you have nothing to worry about." If you follow the arrow through yes, you're lead to a second question box: "Can you do something about the problem?" Once again, for this question box two answers are provided. Answering yes, which means you know a solution, leads you to a box that says "Then you have nothing to worry about." Funnily enough, the answer no, indicating you can't think of a solution, *also* leads you to a box that says the exact same thing: "Then you have nothing to worry about."

The point of the diagram is to illustrate that, once you know whether or not there is anything you can do about a problem, then there really is no point to worrying about it either way. Although the diagram seems like a clever joke about life, it actually makes a very important hidden point: sometimes the greatest amount of worrying we go through is a result of having to answer that second question: "Can you do something about the problem?"

This is a hard question to answer because it requires you to forecast possible outcomes of taking various actions or not taking any. Since this involves a great deal of uncertainty, which is draining to the body and mind (see page 73), deciding how to move forward can be very difficult, which is the very thing that makes problems problematic. A lack of knowledge makes the future hard to discern. As Herman Melville explained, "Ignorance is the parent of fear." In fact, that's exactly why people tend to be afraid of the dark and of giving speeches, because both of those things involve a great deal of uncertainty, which shadows our ability to anticipate the immediate future.

What Herman Melville failed to explain is that ignorance is also the parent of faith. In this context, the word faith does not necessarily take on religious meaning, but simply refers to a principle of action and power. Faith is simply moving forward and doing so without perfect knowledge about how things will turn out. When you walk out the door in the morning, you don't *know* that the knob will turn and that the door will swing open on its hinges and shut nicely behind you, but you proceed anyway, and do so on good faith. In other words, opening a door is an act of faith.

When it comes to solving problems, the best attitude to have is a faithful one. Simply move forward, with trust in yourself and in your ability to exercise good judgment to overcome life's challenges, recognizing that it's always darkest before dawn.

DISCUSSION QUESTION
↝ Have you ever thought about faith in a non-religious way? As a principle of action?
ACTION ITEM
↝ Identify a problem you have been worrying about and reflect on it with a faithful attitude.
FOLLOW-UP
↝ Schedule a discussion about your reflection with a helping-professional you like and trust.

Grow Your Intelligence

Because so much information has been circulated about the importance of IQ as it relates to success, many people have gotten the wrong idea that intelligence is a fixed characteristic, that doesn't change much throughout the course of life. This is actually a terrible myth that has nothing to do with actual science.

Research shows that individuals are not only able to develop their intelligence, but that the brain will actually change and grow to accommodate that intelligence. For one example, research conducted by Dr. Craig Kinsley at Richmond University has indicated that female rats can actually increase their memory and learning ability simply by becoming mothers, which increases the size of certain areas of their brains.[8] Whether you're a rat or a human, going through challenging experiences, like giving birth or fulfilling the responsibilities of motherhood, is actually what can cause our brain to improve itself, just like working-out a muscle.

Challenging muscles with ever increasing resistance causes them to be broken down and built back up even stronger. Our minds work exactly the same way. As we encounter new and interesting challenges, our mind grows and adapts to achieve success and overcome setbacks. These changes within our mind occur conceptually, but also physically within the neural framework of our brains, just like a muscle that grows over time.

Students should feel encouraged to challenge themselves in order to achieve mental growth. While the fact that you can improve your intelligence may seem fairly straight forward, many people have grown up believing the myth that, when it comes to intelligence, you've either got it or you don't. Hopefully, realizing that this just isn't true will help students to see that potential is really about hard work over time, not just about ability.

Stanford University researcher Lisa Blackwell developed a handout entitled "You Can Grow Your Intelligence"[9] that can be used to facilitate a discussion about these issues. The handout is available online and linked on the resources page of *www.studysimpler.com*.

DISCUSSION QUESTION

> ❧ Have you ever bought into the myth that some people are just smart and others aren't?

ACTION ITEM

> ❧ Locate the handout mentioned above and share it with a friend to see how they react.

FOLLOW-UP

> ❧ Schedule a discussion about your experience with a helping-professional you like and trust.

All Diplomas Look the Same

In the winter of 2003, Merrilee Webb, a professor of music and expert in the field of education, found herself somewhat disappointed in the efforts of her students in one of her music education classes. She had assigned the class a fairly simple set of homework assignments, which very few of the students were completing on a regular basis and which even fewer were completing with much quality.

In an effort to remind her students of their duty to themselves and of the personally meaningful nature of their education, she postponed class one day to give them a short talk. She wanted them to change their behavior, but knew it was even more important for her students to want to change themselves. She started by pointing out that every student in that class was going to finish their university degree and be given their diploma—a piece of paper that in appearance would look exactly identical to every other one given out.

"Everyone's piece of paper looks the same," she said earnestly, "but not everyone's piece of paper means the same thing."

"Only you will know what you put into your piece of paper," she continued. "To everyone else, it will look the exactly the same."

The students thought about the original assignments that they had been given and realized that the homework hadn't been given out as busy work; the work was assigned to give them experience and to help them to grow. And now they were feeling guilty about neglecting that work and, in turn, neglecting the quality of their own education.

"Be careful with what you put into your piece of paper," she concluded, "because you're the only one who has to live with it."

The message stuck and the students changed. More of them submitted their work on time and more of them submitted work of a higher quality. They all graduated. They all received the same piece of paper. And each of them knew what theirs meant.

Ten years later, at least one of her students still remembers that lesson and how important it was to him and how greatly it inspired his life. As Michelangelo once said, "My best work is in my best interest."

DISCUSSION QUESTION

✎ What aspects of your progress towards graduation are you particularly pleased about so far?

ACTION ITEM

✎ Make a list of all the things that you want your diploma to mean when you finish college.

FOLLOW-UP

✎ Share that list with friends or even faculty members using social media, email, or in person.

Fixed Mindset vs. Growth Mindset

Stanford University psychologist Carol Dweck has performed some fascinating research that indicates that individuals either experience what she calls Growth Mindset or Fixed Mindset, which has a drastic effect on how well they are able to perform in challenging settings. Dr. Dweck outlines these principles in her book *Mindset*,[10] which is a must read for educators and students alike.

Growth Mindset is the understanding that you do not have to be good at something right from the start in order to get better. Growth oriented individuals are willing to try new things, understand that change occurs over time, and don't get upset in the face of opposition.[10]

Conversely, individuals with Fixed Mindset see themselves as unchangeable and unable to improve their skills. Even if they are talented, Fixed oriented individuals feel that their abilities are not going to change much and are insecure if they don't live up to the standards that they have set for themselves (believing that failure is not something that can be overcome). For individuals who are less talented, Fixed Mindset causes them to resist the idea that their abilities can be developed through hard work.[10]

In one experiment, Dr. Dweck found that children that were praised for their performance with compliments that emphasized their inherent *abilities* ("You're so smart!"), rather than their good *effort* ("You really worked hard on that and it paid off!"), were far more likely to engage in subsequent tasks from a Fixed Mindset, rather than a Growth Mindset. In other words, ability-based praised, which emphasizes fixed talents over hard work, actually enables students to devalue hard work and expect successful results as an extension of minimal effort. Interestingly, when subsequently offered the choice to continue working on easy or more challenging problems, those who were praised for their abilities were far more likely to choose the easier problems out of fear of losing their personal image of success. Conversely, those who were praised with effort-based compliments were more likely to choose to work on challenging problems, which they perceived as an engaging opportunity for growth. In other words, they were more likely to understand that you can actually grow your intelligence through facing and working-through challenging situations (see page 66).[10]

While these topics could be summarized further here, Dr. Dweck's book does a much better job at explaining the differences between these two drastically different Mindsets and is something that can be read in just two or three days. Additionally, a handout related to these issues and linked on the resources page of *www.studysimpler.com* can be used to facilitate a discussion about Mindset.

DISCUSSION QUESTION

    ❧ Do you think you have more of a Growth or Fixed Mindset when it comes to academics?

ACTION ITEM

    ❧ Purchase and read "Mindset" by Carol Dweck or borrow it from your campus library.

FOLLOW-UP

    ❧ Take notes about what stands out to you in the book. Share your notes using social media.

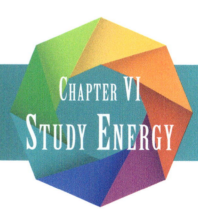

CHAPTER VI
STUDY ENERGY

Glucose & Self-Regulation

Many people mistakenly believe that IQ (Intelligence Quotient) is a good indicator of whether or not someone will be successful in school or even in life. While IQ does influence these outcomes, it is not a terribly great indicator of overall well-being, especially when compared to an individual's ability to work hard and self-regulate.

Self-regulation is the capacity to resist giving in to a natural or desirable impulse in preference for a more long term or more meaningful reward or benefit. For example, in the famous Stanford marshmallow study, 5-year-olds were each given a single marshmallow and told that, although they could choose to eat this first marshmallow whenever they'd like, if they would refrain from eating the marshmallow for 15 minutes while the researcher left the room, they would receive a second marshmallow upon the researcher's return. Some children couldn't wait, while others were successful in holding out.[1]

This study followed these children into adulthood and found that, remarkably, children who demonstrated self-regulation during the marshmallow scenario continued to exercise good self-regulation throughout their lives: they achieved higher SAT scores, higher levels of educational attainment, and higher levels of ability to cope with frustration and stress.[1]

Other research, conducted by Roy Baumeister and his colleagues at Florida State University, has clearly demonstrated that self-regulation relies on glucose as a limited supply of energy. One study clearly showed that:

"(a) acts of self-control reduce blood glucose levels,

"(b) low levels of blood glucose after an initial self-control task predicted poor performance on a subsequent self-control task, and

"(c) initial acts of self-control impaired performance on subsequent self-control tasks, but consuming a glucose drink eliminated these impairments."[2]

Basically, if an individual's blood glucose level is low and you put them through the marshmallow experiment, they will be less able to hold out for the second mallow. These findings stress the importance of fueling success through appropriate diet and productive self-regulatory habits, such as regular exercise and other healthy choices, so that when destructive distractions present themselves, self-regulatory resources (in the form of blood glucose) are abundantly available.

DISCUSSION QUESTION

ↄ Have you ever noticed yourself getting grumpy when you're hungry or tired?

ACTION ITEM

ↄ Identify one thing that you currently have a hard time self-regulating against.

FOLLOW-UP

ↄ Make a resolution to self-regulate that one area. Announce your resolution on social media.

Fuel Proper Study Habits

Once an individual realizes how important blood glucose is to self-regulation (see previous page), they might start getting ideas about how to fuel their self-regulatory energy for their academic well being. Listening to lectures, reading academic texts, and working during study sessions requires a great deal of self-regulation and energy. The rewards of academic life rarely feel immediate and so even good students have to constantly battle off distractions and a desire to disengage from learning. Since every instance of self-regulation depletes a limited supply of self-regulatory resources (blood glucose), determining which sources of energy are more effective than others is crucial to academic well-being.

Sugary drinks (even 100% juice!) and convenient snack foods may seem like they provide the needed energy, but they tend to spike glucose for only a short period of time before causing a crash. As such, more complex and fibrous carbohydrates, which take longer to digest and provide a steady release of energy over time, are far more desirable. A recent experiment conducted by twin doctors Alexander and Chris Van Tulleken demonstrated that, while consuming carbs may not help with maintaining a trim figure, they have a dramatic positive impact on our ability to think clearly and remain alert.[3] The most readily available sources of complex, fibrous carbohydrates are whole grains, vegetables, and whole pieces of fruit, including apples, oranges, plums, pears, berries, peaches, and so forth.

As for beverages, while fruit juice is extremely healthy compared to other energy drinks, the relatively high levels of fructose (which have to be metabolized by the liver) and the absence of fiber causes juice to be less healthy than unprocessed, whole fruit. For a productive study session, eat more complex carbohydrates two to three hours beforehand (whole grains and vegetables) and less complex carbohydrates immediately before and during (whole pieces of fruit). When this type of nutrition is not available, relying on a 100% fruit and vegetable juice blend can be a good alternative, especially when short on time.

DISCUSSION QUESTION

⮞ How would you rate your current strategies of fueling your study sessions?

ACTION ITEM

⮞ Eat an apple during the middle of a particularly long study session. Note the effect this has.

FOLLOW-UP

⮞ Schedule a discussion about this experience with a helping-professional you like and trust.

Uncertainty and Energy Levels

As is explained on the two previous pages, energy levels are drastically reduced by engaging in self-regulation, or staying task-oriented in the face of debilitating distractions. Interestingly, something else that drastically reduces our blood glucose (energy) levels is uncertainty.

As explained by Jessica Alquist, in her dissertation entitled "What You Don't Know Can Hurt You,"[4] uncertainty actually impairs our ability to self-regulate effectively. This impairment reduces our mental energy levels by sapping the resources (blood glucose) that would otherwise be available to other mental processes. In fact, as Alquist discovered, "uncertainty impaired self-control even more than certainty of a negative outcome."[4]

There are so many things in students' lives that could cause uncertainty and subsequently have a negative impact on their ability to self-regulate and to be mentally focused. For example, while personal relationships seems to occupy a completely separate domain than academics, an ongoing troubled relationship with lots of unpredictable elements could be the very thing that is causing an individual's grades to begin to suffer. Many people have probably experienced this kind of distracting and debilitating uncertainty without realizing that there is actually a scientific explanation to why it causes so much trouble in their lives: as energy is rerouted to dealing with interpersonal uncertainty, fewer resources are available to focusing on the things that matter to academic success.

Students should be especially careful about dealing with uncertainty in their lives and do as much as they can to avoid going through long periods of uncertainty that would consume up the mental resources they should be devoting to school. If forced to endure such long periods of uncertainty, which can be a fairly common possibility, students can supplement their energy levels by eating pieces of whole fruit or by drinking healthy fruit juice on a regular basis, even six or eight times a day.

In a very serious way, uncertainty causes a big drop in our ability to focus and think clearly about what we really need to be working on in order to achieve academic success. Fortunately, when feeling uncertain, doing something as simple as drinking a glass of juice can actually reverse the effects of the uncertainty by restoring our blood glucose levels and returning us to our normal level of functioning.

DISCUSSION QUESTION

&rarrcurvearrowleft; What types of uncertainty have you found yourself facing as a student?

ACTION ITEM

&rarrcurvearrowleft; Make a list of uncertainty in other areas of your life, even if they seem unrelated to school.

FOLLOW-UP

&rarrcurvearrowleft; With the aid of a helping-professional, identify connections between your list and school.

The Myth about Coffee & Energy Drinks

You've probably heard someone (maybe even yourself) say, "I have to have my coffee in the morning; it gives me so much energy." While this statement seems to be true, it's actually a trick of the senses. By in large, unless you've added a terribly large amount of cream and sugar to your coffee, it's actually providing you with less than 15 calories, so it's not adding much energy (calories) to the system at all. Instead, it's actually causing you to use *more* energy.

The perception that caffeine gives us more energy stems from the reality that caffeine causes one to *use* more energy—something you can really feel! Caffeine stimulates the adrenal glands to release adrenaline, which spikes activity in the sympathetic nervous system: heart rate increases, more blood circulates, respiration increases, and an acute sense of alertness (or even mild paranoia) ensues. Adrenaline is meant to help one cope with unexpected challenges, such as an attacking lion jumping out from behind a bush.

Interestingly, because the effects of caffeine are easily perceived, individuals report that this spike in energy *usage* is actually highly beneficial, even necessary to their everyday lives. However, research has shown that post-caffeine energy levels in coffee drinkers are no higher than energy levels in individuals that do not drink coffee.[5] This is largely due to the fact that caffeine is a stimulant and something to which the body can develop tolerance. Tolerance occurs when ever-increasing levels of a substance are required to achieve the same effect. For example, when a person becomes addicted to drugs, taking the same amount each time actually produces less and less of an effect. This means that the addict constantly has to take greater and greater doses to achieve the same high.

What makes this process much worse is that, as tolerance sets in, the absence of the stimulant causes withdrawal effects to occur, resulting in recurring crashes. This means that the individual eventually has to partake of the substance *just to feel normal*. As a result of these effects, individuals that drink coffee on a regular basis are actually in a state of chronic adrenal fatigue: ever increasing usage of caffeine has caused their supply of adrenaline to be consistently used up and constantly running on empty.

At the heart of this issue and of the myth that caffeine increases energy is the idea that *using* energy is the same thing as *having* energy. Metaphorically, to compare the body to a power grid, it is as if caffeine turns on so many lights and appliances within a house ("Look how much energy I have!") that the coal gets entirely burned up at the power plant. The house uses up a lot of energy, but doesn't actually have access to any *more* energy than it did to begin with. *Having* more energy only occurs with caloric intake (adding coal to the fire at the plant), like when you eat a piece of fruit. This is like adding wattage to the grid, even if the lights at the house don't get noticeably brighter. When the energy is needed, however, it is ready to be used. Metabolizing actual food increases blood glucose levels, which, although not nearly as exhilarating as a hit of caffeine (because you can't actually feel it happening), is far more healthy in the long run. When adding calories to the system, one can honestly say, "I love fruit! It gives me so much energy!"

The best way to visualize this is using the following diagram. The straight line represents baseline energy levels, perhaps how you might normally feel when you wake up in the morning. The orange line, which consistently remains above the baseline, represents how our energy levels change as we intake and metabolize calories to fuel our energy levels, such as by drinking fruit juice. As the energy we create is used up, we return to baseline energy levels and are prepared to be energized once more in the same way.

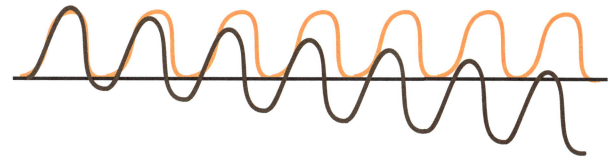

However, when we use caffeine to stimulate the use of energy, the refractory period after each instance is lowered by tolerance and withdrawal effects, represented by the brown line, which slowly moves downward. This means that each subsequent use of caffeine produces a spike in energy that is less than previous instances and much less than simply drinking something like juice. By the time the body reaches the state of adrenal fatigue, represented by the lowest spike in energy on the far right, individuals that regularly consume coffee wake up feeling terrible and have to intake caffeine just to start their day.

Typically, students that have had any long-term experience with caffeine consumption can relate to the diagram above and may react to this discussion in a variety of ways. One particularly common reaction is to ask a confounding question like, "Well, what if a person drinks juice *and* coffee at the same time?! Doesn't that balance everything out?" The purpose of this topic isn't to condemn anyone's behavior or, necessarily, to encourage people to immediately change their habits. Rather, the information is presented to provide greater insight into the principles of how caffeine influences the body so that individuals can make educated decisions. By the way, drinking both doesn't balance everything out.

Frequently, students who interact with this information have a natural desire to shift away from the use of caffeine in preference for more efficient energy solutions. This is an encouraging response to the material, but one that must be engaged with caution. Reversing the effects of tolerance and withdrawal can take up to as much as six weeks. As one student named Mark quickly found out, shifting away from caffeine isn't something that should be attempted right in the middle of a quarter or semester, as fatigue and irritability can quickly set in. Rather, he decided to wait until winter break to make the transition, which was a far more sensible strategy than quitting cold-turkey.

DISCUSSION QUESTION

   ↪ How hard do you think it would be for a person to stop using coffee as a "source" of energy?

ACTION ITEM

   ↪ Based on the information provided above, design an Action Item that will work for you.

FOLLOW-UP

   ↪ Discuss the results of your self-created Action Item with a friend or helping-professional.

Sleep

Everyone acknowledges the importance of getting a good night's sleep, especially before a test, however many students struggle to achieve this goal, even with the best of intentions. There are a few helpful hints that can make a big difference in feeling well rested and making the most of the sleep that we do get.

In the same way that place cells cue our bodies and minds to prepare to engage in certain activities when we are in certain environments (see page 23), certain behaviors, like having a bedtime routine, can also cue our bodies to prepare for more restful sleep. Theoretically, routines help the body prepare for restful sleep through the process of classical conditioning, which causes the mind to pair certain smells, events, sounds, textures, and other elements of the routine with the sensation of falling asleep. For example, if you wear the same type of pajamas to sleep every night, the feel of the material can help your body be cued to fall asleep. The purpose of using such routines is to 1) fall asleep faster, 2) awake fewer times in the night, and 3) wake feeling more rested.

Another problem many individuals have is waking up on time. We live in a society where waking up to an alarm is fairly customary, however, doing so is not nearly as pleasant as waking up naturally. Sleeping with the blinds open to let in the morning light results in a more natural waking process. Light streaming in the window activates the body's wake cycle, allowing the individual to wake feeling rested, rather than groggy. Waking up early actually seems to be a critical factor related to student success. A group of researchers at the University of Illinois found that "Of all the variables considered, sleep habits, particularly wake-up times, accounted for the largest amount of variance in grade point averages. Later wake-up times were associated with lower average grades."[6]

Finally, and perhaps most startling of all, the idea that 8-hours of sleep is an ideal amount for everyone is entirely false. Individuals differ drastically in the amount of sleep they require and only trial and error can reveal whether or not you're getting enough. If you are having difficulty waking up in the morning or find that you fall asleep at inappropriate times, you can be sure that you are not getting enough sleep and need to adjust accordingly. Try to sleep for periods of time that are multiples of 1.5 hours, as each REM sleep cycle lasts roughly that long. Similarly, when taking a nap, try to rest for fewer than 20 minutes or at least 1.5 hours to avoid waking feeling groggy.[7]

DISCUSSION QUESTION

- Do you feel like you are getting enough sleep or that you could do better about this?

ACTION ITEM

- Write down a bedtime routine that you'd like to follow for a week. Try it out!

FOLLOW-UP

- Share your experience using social media to encourage your friends to get better sleep, too.

Dreams

While many people dream on a regular basis, few have stopped to consider that those dreams may actually be helping them solve some of the most difficult problems that they have to face.

A fascinating study conducted in 2010 showed that dreams help us to problem solve by continuing to work out problems while we sleep. After assigning participants to work on a complex maze and then take a 90 minute break, researchers found that people who did not take a nap during the break "showed no improvement or did even worse after the break."[8] Similarly, people who took a nap during the break, but woke up reporting no maze-related dreams "did better but showed only marginal improvement."[8] Conversely, participants "who reported dreaming about the maze showed a startling improvement, cutting their completion time in half."[8]

These amazing results are due to the fact that dreaming utilizes the information that is already inside our minds in order to construct new experiences. While those experiences aren't technically 'real,' the mind is still able to learn from them and continue to develop our understanding by making the information that we already have inside of our heads more useful and more organized.

Ultimately, it is not reasonable to expect everyone to take a nap and have a problem-related dream every time they are facing a challenging situation, but this information does lend credence to the idea that taking a break from studying to replenish our energy through a short power nap can have some seriously desirable side-effects. Sleep not only refreshes the mind but may be a perfect environment for the mind to more fully organize and work through information it has been recently exposed to.

Since the research study showed that the dreamers were able to cut their performance time in half, it's perfectly reasonable to assume that problem-related dreaming could easily make the difference between an A or a B on a test. However, it's probably not advisable to try to slip that nap in while you're actually taking the test.

DISCUSSION QUESTION

   ❧ Do you have very many dreams when you sleep or not so much?

ACTION ITEM

   ❧ If you tend to have a lot of dreams, keep a dream journal for just one week.

FOLLOW-UP

   ❧ Share how related you think your dreams are to your academics using social media.

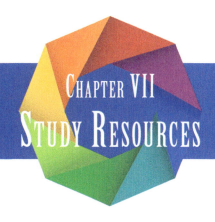

CHAPTER VII
STUDY RESOURCES

Writers' Center

No matter what a student's major is, there will come a time in their academic career when they are faced with a written assignment that seems just a little too tough to tackle. Most universities offer some kind of writing support in the form of a resource center where students can take their written work for constructive and holistic feedback. Most writing centers are geared toward helping students develop better writing skills, in addition to getting a better grade on the assignment. Interestingly, because of this dynamic, it is not uncommon for college writing centers to be most frequently used by students who are especially proficient in writing and value feedback as a means of making their writing even better.

Since the service is typically free, the only barrier that most students will face in attempting to use this resource will simply be setting aside enough time to take in a written assignment for feedback. This also means that writing the paper a few days before the deadline is imperative in order to allow enough time to schedule an appointment. Making several appointments at your university's writing center, especially early in your academic career, can actually save you time later on as you learn to become an ever more proficient writer of academic papers.

Disability Support Services

Modern universities recognize that not all students are able to engage their academic work in the most typical way as a result of some temporary or long term disability (whether physical or mental in nature). While most students with significant disabilities are well-acquainted with the services that are available to them, many other students with less severe disabilities, such as test anxiety, dyslexia, or dyscalculia, might not be aware that universities are willing to provide certain accommodations to students in order to help them succeed.

For example, a common service provided by a disability support center is for people who break their dominant hand. Many universities will actually pay another student to take notes on behalf of the temporarily disabled student, so that they can continue to be successful. Similarly, if a student is experiencing some kind of medical set-back, temporary accommodations can frequently be arranged through the disability support office, in addition to arrangements that students can make with their faculty members.

As a student, if you, for any reason, suspect that you are experiencing some kind of temporary or long term mental or physical disability that is affecting or will affect your ability to perform as a student, do not hesitate to seek out the disability support office on your campus.

Career Services

The most interesting thing about the career office on campus is that their services include help for students that goes well beyond just picking a career and finding a job. The best example of this is that many career advisors are able to help students with one of the biggest challenges that university students face: picking a major. In fact, the best time to stop into career services for the first time is not as a junior or senior, when you're finally deciding on a career, but near the end of your freshman year. During this first appointment, you can get a head start on some of the most important details about finding a career and ensure that the major you select is truly a good fit for your career goals.

Career advisors not only have many tools at their disposal that assess what careers students might be interested in or naturally talented at, but also can help students decided which majors will help them achieve those goals. Additionally, career services are not only about helping you find a job after you graduate. Career advisors recognize the importance of having a valuable work history and can help you locate local jobs that fit your career path and interests while you're still in school.

As part of some of their most helpful services, career advisors can also help you learn how to write, structure, and effectively submit resumes and cover letters. Perhaps the best part about career services is that their resources tend to be absolutely free.

TRiO Advising & McNair Scholars

The United States Department of Education offers free advising services to students who come from low-income households, who are first-generation college students, or who have a registered disability. These services are called TRiO Student Support Services and students all over the nation who have taken advantage of this program have nothing but good things to say about the difference that TRiO has made in their lives.

Even if you are already meeting with a general undergraduate advisor or program advisor, if you qualify for TRiO services, you should also make an appointment to meet with a TRiO advisor in the near future to discuss the services that are available to you through the program.

Additionally, for students who are interested in attending graduate school, the TRiO McNair Scholars program is designed to provide the necessary preparation that is crucial to getting accepted into the best programs around the country. If you qualify for TRiO services and are interested in attending graduate school, joining the McNair Scholars program is one of the absolute best things that you can do to qualify yourself for success.

Counseling Services

Most universities provide some kind of free psychological counseling services to students as a way to help keep student energy focused on academic success. Many people have the false notion that counseling services are only for mentally unstable individuals, but the reality is that these services are for everyone.

Counseling has been designed to provide clients with an experience to talk out their most troubling concerns in a safe, supportive environment. People who attend counseling sessions often find that simply opening up about their concerns helps them to think about solutions in a new way.

Since the service tends to be free and includes access to qualified professionals that are dedicated to seeing the student succeed, there are few barriers to trying the service out to see if it is a right fit, especially during especially upsetting times.

Often, while students can have great social support systems, there might be certain topics that they still feel somewhat uncomfortable discussing even within their closest circle of family and friends (who may even be the problem). This is an excellent situation in which students should feel encouraged to make an appointment to see a university counselor.

Tutoring

In addition to the main tutoring office or learning resource center on campus, many departments throughout the university offer additional tutors that are supervised directly by the course faculty. If you are taking an especially difficult course and need support in addition to what is offered at the main tutoring center, consider asking the departmental office or your faculty member if the department offers tutoring.

Some of the most likely departments to offer in-house tutoring are mathematics, chemistry, and physics, due to those courses being especially difficult for many students to master. Other departments that are likely to offer tutoring are those that are related to math reasoning like economics and accounting.

Since tutoring can be an especially expensive service if paid for out-of-pocket, students should feel encouraged to access any free tutoring services that are available.

khanacademy.org

In 2006, a graduate of MIT and Harvard Business School, Sal Khan decided to start making short online tutoring videos in his spare time. His explanations turned out to be surprisingly straightforward and helpful to students across the world. As a result of his success on the project, The Gates Foundation decided to fund khanacademy.org as a full enterprise, rather than something Sal Khan just did as a past time. The videos cover a wide variety of subjects and are provided free of charge.

Currently there are over 4,500 searchable videos in nearly every university subject that you can think of. The videos last roughly 10-20 minutes and flow together to make up the building blocks of a larger series of instructional concepts. Students interested in using the service can watch the videos before going to lecture to get a preview of the material or use the videos after their course lectures to get a second viewpoint. The videos can also be used to supplement tutoring sessions, as needed.

Online Tutoring

Many institutions offer online tutoring as a free service that tends to be available during nights and weekends, in addition to typical business hours. This schedule has the advantage of providing tutoring services during times when students are more likely to be completing their homework. It is also a great tool for getting answers to quick questions that can easily be discussed over the internet.

Many online tutoring services are more than just a chat service and include fully interactive skype-like video and voice sessions, in addition to providing the tutor with a digital whiteboard onto which they can draw out concepts, which are then visible to the student. If this service is used on a regular basis, the user-interface becomes like second nature to the student and fades into the background of getting the understanding that is needed.

Academic Software

During the past 10 years, a huge array of academic-oriented programs and applications have been released to the market to help students succeed. There are far too many to discuss in detail, but in this technological age, students should feel empowered to explore the options that are most consonant with their needs and academic styles. Some of the most popular programs and applications include *Dragon Naturally Speaking, Read and Write Gold 10, Grammarly*, and *Notability*. Typically, more information about each of these programs is available through each service's website.

Chapter VIII

The Tutor Guide

The Tutor Guide

The introduction to this manual outlines various principles of effective student engagement during the process of implementing *Study Simpler* as an intervention model, but fails to address effective principles of how to assist students with their homework, a topic that is frequently coupled with study skills development. Since, on most university campuses, tutors primarily fill the role of helping with homework, Chapter 8 is primarily discussed in terms of tutor pedagogy, although other helping-professionals may benefit from its contents, as well.

The roles that a tutor must juggle can be quite demanding given the wide array of needs that students seek to address through the process of tutoring. What would seem on the surface to be a very straightforward profession, being a tutor can often seem more like dynamic blend of friend, guardian, task-master, sounding-board, mentor, peer, advocate, counselor, and even that person who, in a very simple way, changes the lives of those they serve. As tutors navigate these constantly shifting demands on their professional identities, many have quickly surmised that there is more to helping students with coursework than simply helping the students with coursework.

Using *Study Simpler,* tutors can feel encouraged to incorporate discussion of study skills development into their sessions with students. When done in an effective manner, tutoring sessions become a means by which students are guided in their quest for acquiring better learning skills, in addition to fulfilling a secondary role of allowing the tutor to be a co-navigator of the course material. By implementing the *Simpler* model in this way, tutoring should not only aid the student in the course for which they are seeking help, but should also spill over into how they approach the material of other courses as well. Through this more holistic approach to tutoring, "Tutor the student and not the subject..." becomes more than just a mantra for success, but a template for empowering the tutor to engage the student about study skills development using brief discussions on a wide variety of topics. *Simpler* tutoring sessions cease being strictly material-focused and are more effectively recast as fundamentally *student*-focused.

The nature of the *Simpler* intervention model requires at least a 10% commitment of time towards study skill development to every 90% that is devoted to the course material (roughly 5 minutes out of a 50 minute session). This is an absolute maximum, as spending too much time on study skills development can actually be terribly detrimental to student progress. Prioritizing the holistic discussion of study skills to occur during the *first* 5 minutes of a tutoring session is typically a good idea, since the pathway that a tutoring session can take may easily cause the tutor and student to lose track of time. Establishing this expectation in the mind of tutors and students alike is critical to the effectiveness of using the *Simpler* model in connection with tutoring, as students may resist the process if not initially and fully established as the ongoing reality.

Self-Efficacy

In the book *Social Foundations of Thought and Action*,[1] Albert Bandura, a preeminent psychologist and Stanford University professor, introduced the concept of self-efficacy. Self-efficacy is the idea that any given individual has a certain sense or awareness of their ability to cope with and overcome challenging circumstances, given their own unique skills and capacities. As Bandura explains, some students have high self-efficacy, which is the *belief* that they have the ability to perform well. It is important to note that this is different than high *ability*. Having high self-efficacy allows students to cope with challenging situations effectively and, as a result, achieve better life outcomes. In contrast, other students, even some of the most competent, suffer from the debilitating effects of low self-efficacy, which is the belief that they will not perform well. Unfortunately, this often results in a reticence to even try.

Bandura theorized that individuals with high self-efficacy are more willing to engage in new activities, exhibit greater effort and persistence while performing difficult tasks, and have more positive and effective emotional and cognitive experiences while engaged in educational settings.[2] Since most learning involves a great deal of challenge and growth, these individuals tend to cope quite well with difficult circumstances and are more likely to achieve success. On the other side of the coin, poor self-efficacy can lead to outcomes in which students fail to engage in new learning experiences, give up early when challenged, and suffer from negative thoughts and unpleasant emotions during the entire learning process.[2]

Thankfully, as Bandura outlined, self-efficacy can grow and develop through four influential factors: 1) mastery experiences, 2) vicarious experience, 3) verbal persuasion, and 4) experiencing physiological states of confidence.[3] *Study Simpler* was designed to address all four of these areas through interaction that encourage students to progressively incorporate various strategies and principles into their academic approach.

Mastery experiences are those in which the student performs well and experiences a sense of accomplishment as a result of the completion of a meaningful task. As tutors work with students to develop better study habits and as those study habits are implemented with successful results (mastery), students' sense of self-efficacy will begin to grow. This growth is essential because, while the student may or may not be acquiring the course material in a way that instills personal confidence, most can quickly acquire and successfully implement newly discovered study habits in a way that provides them with a much-needed sense of mastery.

Vicarious experiences are those in which the student is able to see another person effectively engage in a target behavior to achieve success. This kind of modeling is an essential part of social learning and a critical element to the dynamics that can make the *Simpler* model work in both the lives of the students and of the tutors. Since students are more readily able to learn by example, tutors who practice the strategies and principles contained within *Study Simpler* in their own academic lives will be more able to act as vicarious models for students to emulate. In fact, many tutors who have been trained using *Study Simpler* have reported that the information it contains has been at least as helpful to their own lives as to their role as tutors.

Tutors should also feel encouraged to engage in verbal persuasion to help students develop their sense of self-efficacy. A simple "You've got this! I believe in you!" can go a long way to helping a student work up the confidence to face a particularly difficult challenge. Constantly revisiting the subject of study skills development can be an opportunity for tutors to provide this type of needed encouragement and persuasion for students to keep up the good work.

As students achieve success with study skills development and, subsequently, with the course material, they will also begin to feel physiological states of confidence that Bandura described as being so necessary to the development of self-efficacy. Such feelings are a fluid commodity in the realm of student development and can help shield and insulate students from feelings of frustration and helplessness in other domains of their lives as well.

In this way, study skills development becomes a critical tool for growth in both students and tutors alike. Indeed, as tutors see their students succeeding through the study skills processes that they have implemented, their own sense of self-efficacy is also likely to grow and develop in turn. This is exactly the kind of meaningful outcome that the *Simpler* model was designed to produce, through an ever increasing awareness of personal capacity within both the student and the tutor to succeed as a result of purposeful effort.

Social Intelligence vs. Pedagogy

People with high levels of social intelligence enjoy interpersonal interaction and are typically excellent at discerning how to provide effective explanations. They tend not to shrink at opportunities to speak in front of others and generally enjoy spending long periods of time engaged in conversation. All of these characteristics lend themselves well to the roles that a tutor must consistently fulfill. In fact, many sociable individuals seek employment as tutors due to their interpersonally oriented natures.

Unusually, social intelligence can also be an Achilles' heel for tutors who fail to place pedagogical concerns above social graces. Pedagogy, or the art of instruction, often finds itself at curious odds with social intelligence, simply because what is socially intelligent is not always effective for purposes of instruction. Although effective pedagogy does not always find itself at odds with social intelligence, it must be given preference if truly stellar tutoring is to occur.

As an example, silence between two people during an ongoing interaction is frequently antithetical to social conventions. Socially intelligent individuals are typically quick to fill such pauses with verbalization, especially if the silence occurs as a response to a question. Indeed, research has shown that most instructors wait less than 3 seconds before interjecting to fill silence after asking a question,[4] without realizing that 3-6 seconds is the typically required time to think of an answer and move to speak.[5] Tutors who have especially sharp social perceptions may find themselves interjecting to fill silence too often and too quickly. This silence, while socially unusual, is typically a sign of productive cognition.

As another example of the importance of pedagogy over social considerations, many tutors and students will work through course concepts on scratch paper or even directly onto the students' assignments in order to be efficient. The latter of these options presents serious questions of academic integrity and issues of ethical professionalism. While working through concepts on paper seems

89

reasonable, even desirable for students who want to keep a record of their interactions with the tutor, this can be an unintentional, yet subtle way of undermining student responsibility for the work. This issue is particularly problematic because students can inadvertently use session notes as a way of demonstrating knowledge on assignments that isn't entirely theirs.

In contrast, the prevalence of whiteboards and, on some campuses, even whiteboard tables, provides an alternative that can be effectively used to steer students away from the pitfall of relying too heavily on notes written by tutors. Working through problems on whiteboards and finding solutions that can be quickly erased before being copied down encourages students to actually learn the concepts and processes, rather than focusing on recording the solutions alone. While not terribly socially intelligent, due to students' desire to keep session notes, using and erasing a whiteboard surface is a sound pedagogical practice.

A related aspect of pedagogical proficiency is ensuring that the students become active in the building of their own knowledge. Allison King, professor of education at California State University, authored a seminal article[6] on the importance of reducing the time spent lecturing students entitled "From Sage on the Stage to Guide on the Side." Her writing not only outlines the importance of transitioning from a sage-like dispensing of knowledge to a more guide-oriented approach, but also provides a variety of suggested learning activities to facilitate this process, such as having students make predictions about the material, generate their own examples of homework problems, draw connections to real-world examples, and pair up with classmates to dialogue about concepts.[6]

While many tutors might intuitively feel that their role is to be a personal lecturer, this is actually counter to principles of effective tutor pedagogy, even though many students may disagree. In tutoring sessions, emphasizing the student's responsibility for engagement can make the difference between a positive educational environment and one that mimics ineffective classrooms. While students may encourage tutors to simply re-explain the lecture or textbook material, resisting this type of exchange is critical. Although it may not be the most popular approach to tutoring, creating a learning environment in which the *student's* progression through the material is paramount enables them to own their educational experiences. Since tutoring is meant to be fundamentally different from the classroom experience, ensuring that the session is run in a more student-centered manner, rather than a content-centered manner is the difference between tutoring that conforms to social conventions and tutoring that upholds sound principles of pedagogy. As students who perceive this discrepancy have explained, "I thought tutoring was going to be helpful; instead I just got another lecture."

As tutors remain committed to pedagogical concerns over social conventions, their ability to effectively balance both socially intelligent responses and effective instructional methods will naturally mature. Over time, most tutors will develop a unique, personal blend of the two strengths, dynamically balanced against one another.

Modeling Coping with Ignorance

A common and grave fear experienced by many new tutors is that they will be asked a question about the material that they do not happen to know the answer to. While such a scenario is actually commonplace in the world of tutoring, tutors can rest assured that the experience is nothing to be afraid of. Primarily, tutors can be secure in knowing that, although society's impressions of their role may differ, a tutor is not meant to be an expert, but simply a more knowledgeable helping figure. As such, when presented with a question that has an unknown answer, the course of action most immediately useful to the tutor is not an evasive or vague explanation, but, rather, a sincere and enthusiastic, "I don't happen to know, but let's see if we can look it up and figure it out…"

In fact, while many tutors intuitively feel that their role is to be fairly equipped in their knowledge of the given course material, it is actually far more important for them to be readily equipped in study skills, research skills, inquiry habits, and appropriately positive attitudes about academic engagement. The demonstration of effective research and inquiry skills is actually a wonderful opportunity for the student to discover that they are not alone in having to deal with occasional bouts of ignorance. Further, an enthusiastic, positive response from the tutor in such circumstances models the importance of engaging the state of not knowing something with an attitude of discovery, rather than with discouragement. Frequently, resources that are employed rather intuitively by tutors to investigate unknown aspects of the material—such as the glossary, index, reference manuals, etc.—are completely foreign tools to students, who may have never even been expected to rely on them. These resources include, but are not limited to, class notes, the professor (during office hours), the text book and its full range of reference materials, online search engines, classmates, study groups, online tutorial videos, practice tests, and supplemental instruction sessions offered on campus.

Tutors can not only be enthusiastic about using such resources to discover unknown facts and principles, but can also begin to transition responsibility for using these tools to the student. For example, the tutor may initiate the modeling process by accessing the material with the text book in their own hands. During a following instance, they may place the text book in front of and facing the student and ask them to locate the correct explanatory resource. Finally, the tutor can resort to simply prompting the student that some reference resource is an appropriate tool given their current lack of understanding. Students who are expected to effectively use supplementary resources will naturally begin to refer to them automatically, without being prompted. Ultimately, tutoring is a process that, if done correctly, comes to a close with the student feeling readily capable of overcoming moments of confusion with a fully mobilized capacity for inquiry and discovery using available resources.

Three Magic Questions

While there are many threats to a students' academic well being, three in particular seem to be at the core of many student struggles: poor class attendance, poor notetaking skills, and a failure to read the text book. Amazingly, because of these deficiencies, when encountering a particularly difficult homework problem or assignment many students fail to effectively reflect on the course lectures, make a close examination of their notes, or reference the text for greater clarity. This is particularly problematic because, with very few, highly unusual exceptions, nearly everything students are expected to know in order to achieve success in a course (barring prerequisite knowledge) is customarily presented in class or appears in the text.

Three "magic" questions can readily address these concerns and simultaneously reinforce the need for the student to take initial, direct responsibility for their academic well-being. When a student presents their struggles with a given homework problem or assignment, these questions can be introduced as a way to begin to explore their level of academic engagement:

1. Tell me a little bit about what your instructor presented during class about this topic; what do you remember?

2. What do your notes say about these concepts? Can you find a section about this topic?

3. Have you checked your text book for related information regarding these issues?

While many answers are possible and will reveal various aspects of the student's current level of functioning, these questions are only meant to be a starting point for further discussion. Often, they reveal what the student already understands about the material and also act as a mechanism for discerning their level of dedication to effective study habits. Answers may reveal poor course attendance (whether physical or mental in nature), poor notetaking strategies, or ineffective engagement of the text. If these realities present themselves, tutors can not only use the opportunity to help the students understand the course content, but do so in a way that emphasizes the importance of attending class, productive notetaking, and adequate use of the text.

Repeated use of the questions in an effective way will usually result in students including the answers to these questions in their initial explanations of their struggles with the course material. Indeed, students that answer all three questions honestly, and in a way that shows they've already exhausted these avenues, simultaneously validate their need for greater assistance from a more knowledgeable source. Finally, the questions are not meant to be a nuisance or to act as a blockade to the needed assistance, although responsible and irresponsible students alike may see them that way if the tutor engages student answers with enmity. To avoid these outcomes, the questions must be phrased sincerely, rather than rhetorically, and as a means of actually gathering information, rather than making a point. While these questions are not truly "magical," if used effectively they act as one simple tool in the arsenal of techniques that tutors can safely rely on.

Gradual Release of Responsibility

During any series of instructional interactions, responsibility should naturally shift over time from the hands of the instructor to the hands of the student. In order to assist educators in properly engaging students in a way that encourages the student's responsibility, four levels of interaction, or stages of learning, were outlined by educators Douglas Fisher and Nancy Frey. At each of the four levels, the responsibility of the helper and the student are clearly defined.[7] Below, the helper's role is listed first and the student's role follows:

1. I Do, You Watch

2. I Do, You Help

3. You Do, I Help

4. You Do, I Watch

Noticeably, the responsibility of the helper decreases with each stage, while the responsibility of the student increases simultaneously in measure. It is also interesting to note that, on most university campuses, instruction primarily takes the form of the first and fourth stages of this model (lecture and testing), while the middle two stages are skipped over entirely. This fact emphasizes the importance of spending as much time as possible within the second and third stages during any given tutoring session.

Another way to represent this concept is using the following diagram, with lines symbolizing each individual's level of responsibility over time:

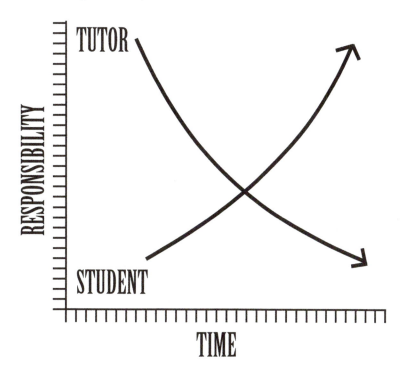

Notice that at no time is the responsibility of either individual reduced to zero, since that is not ultimately the goal of this transitional process. At first, a tutor might need to take more responsibility for the content of the tutoring session as the student orients themselves to the tutoring process. However, as the tutoring process unfolds, this responsibility can slowly be shifted to the student in a manner that not only requires ever greater involvement from the student, but also instills increasing confidence in the material. This model of helping also relies on a gradual, step by step increase in student proficiency. Responsibility can shift in this manner over the course of just one lesson, throughout an entire tutoring session or, generally, over the course of an entire tutoring relationship.

Vgotsky's Zone of Proximal Development

Lev Vgotsky, a 20th century Russian psychologist and educational theorist, pointed out that, while some students may be able to advance from one skill level to the next very quickly, other students may take more time or require additional assistance in order to master the course material. A student's ability to advance from one stage of learning to the next is entirely contingent on the nature of what Vgotsky called the student's Zone of Proximal Development, or "the distance between the actual developmental level as determined by independent problem solving and the level of potential development as determined through problem solving under adult guidance, or in collaboration with more capable peers."[8] Vgotsky called this guidance and collaboration "scaffolding," using the metaphor of a newly constructed building, which needs temporary support until it is ready to stand on its own.

Each student's Zone of Proximal Development is unique to their learning approach and sets the guidepost of how far they can be expected to achieve within the immediate future using the support of scaffolding. Some students have a narrow Zone of Proximal Development, where each step ahead must be taken slowly and carefully to ensure progress. Other students have a more broad Zone of Proximal Development, where leaps and bounds can be made all at once. Interestingly, an individual student's Zone can vary from one subject to another, with one subject needing quite a lot of development time and another not needing much at all.

Regardless of the scope of a student's individual Zone, it is important to remember that there is a certain level at which their current level of progress will become hindered, simply because more time and development is needed to advance their proficiency with the material. In other words, expecting a student to achieve above their personal Zone of Proximal Development can leave them feeling dejected and self-ineffective.

In order to accommodate for individual differences in student progress, fluency checks can be utilized to more fully establish the student's current level of understanding. A fluency check is simply an informal or formal method of determining how well the student understands the material that has been presented so far. Fluency checks should occur rather frequently throughout the course tutoring. Without regularly occurring fluency checks, it can be easy for the tutor to speed along without realizing that they've lost the student in some previously presented step in the material. In other words, they have surpassed the student's Zone of Proximal Development.

Appropriately considering each student's Zone of Proximal Development will ensure that effective pedagogical adjustments are made by the tutors during the tutoring process to accommodate for individual differences amongst students.

A Metaphor for Success

Timmy came running in through the back door to find his mother wiring an electrical socket for their renovation of the kitchen.

"Mom! I cut my arm!" Timmy said as he held up his right arm to present a large gash that was slowly oozing dark, red blood.

"Oh my goodness!" said his mother, rushing over. "What happened?"

"I fell off the ladder leaning up against the shed."

"Well, come over here and we'll fix you up!"

Timmy's mother quickly stopped the bleeding and mended the wound in a way that soothed

Timmy's pain and ensured no scar would appear. Once again, Timmy went out to play and his mother went back to her day's agenda.

Twenty minutes later, Timmy came running in through the back door to find his mother checking pinterest for renovation ideas.

"Mom! I cut my arm!" Timmy said, this time holding up his *left* arm to present a large gash that was slowly oozing dark, red blood.

"You're joking," said his mother in disbelief. "What happened this time?!"

"… I fell off the ladder leaning up against the shed."

His mother suddenly realized that, while she was able to fix the *symptoms* of Timmy's problem, she had done nothing to address Timmy's *actual* problem: his ability to negotiate the ladder leaning up against the shed.

Temporarily effective assistance, while ostensibly helpful, does not always instill that which is necessary for long-term success. At the heart of the entire process of tutoring using *Study Simpler* is the desire to transfer responsibility to the students in a way that helps them avoid the aspects of academic life that lead to poor course outcomes in the first place. In other words, teaching them to fish, which is a skill that remains useful for the duration of their lives, rather than fishing on their behalf, which can only help them from one problematic instance to the next. Using study skills discussions to help students in an ongoing, proactive, and preventative way, rather than relying on single-instances of reactive assistance that simply masks the actual problem, is a crucial element of effectively addressing academic problems, rather than merely suppressing symptoms of poor academic engagement.

Seven Stages of a Productive Tutoring Session

Preparation	• Preparation is important for an effective session • Tutoring cannot be done on "auto-pilot" • Arrive early to get "in the zone" • Prepare worksheets or handouts for sessions

Beginning the Session
 	
5-10 minutes
	1. "Forming"[9]
	  • Build rapport and get to know one another
	
	2. "Norming"[9]
	  • Complete paperwork
	  • Review and establish relevant policies and procedures
	
	3. Dialogue about one Study Skill or Resource during every session
	
	4. Incorporate "Expressed and Assessed Needs"[10] into an Agenda
	  • Expressed Needs: Concepts the student wants to address
	  • Assessed Needs: Other areas of concern assessed by the tutor through holistic discussion of study skills

Working Stage of the Session
 	
30-40 Minutes
	5. Use Active Learning
	  • Emphasize whiteboard-work
	  • Emphasize non-assignment based work
	  • Engage in open-ended, probing questions
	  • Encourage student responsibility
	  • Tutor the student, not the subject

Closing the Session
 	
5-10 Minutes
	6. Recap
	  • Do a brief "wrap up" of materials or information covered
	  • Ask for any final questions for the session
	
	7. Set Expectations
	  • Discuss goals for next session and work that will be completed
	  • Refer student to syllabus to review any upcoming readings or assignments
	  • Confirm your next appointment: day, time, & location

APPENDIX

Key Issues Index

Student complains about...	RELEVANT TOPIC PAGES
❧ ... having too many distractions at home or in their study space.	23, **24**, **25**, 27, **52**, 71, 72, 73
❧ ... running out of energy during study sessions.	24, 26, **31**, 71, **72**, 74, 76
❧ ... making lots of errors on their homework or on tests.	**26**, 31, 45, **48**, 68, 72
❧ ... having their memory go blank as soon as they sit down for a test or quiz.	26, 32, **34**, 43, **45**, **48**, 73
❧ ... how much time they've been spending in the library.	**31**, 37, 72
❧ ... the amount of homework they're expected to complete each day.	26, 31, **33**, **37**, 61
❧ ... their busy schedule.	**33**, 37, 65, 72
❧ ... how much material they are expected to remember for one course.	**32**, **34**, 53, 61, 63
❧ ... disliking their instructor's teaching style.	42, 46, 54, 55, **61**
❧ ... being tested on material that they do not remember the professor discussing in class.	**44**, 61
❧ ... test anxiety.	**45**, **48**, 83, 81
❧ ... how noisy the library is.	**25**, 27, 52
❧ ... the teacher grading too hard or not being very understanding.	38, 55, 60, **61**

Student says "I need..."	RELEVANT TOPIC PAGES
⇜ "... to find a better place to study."	**23**, 24, **25**, 26, 52
⇜ "... to make a schedule, so I can get into a routine."	23, 31, 32, **33**, 34, 35, 37, 62, 76
⇜ "... more time to study."	**32**, **33**, 37, 72
⇜ "... to do better on the next test than I did on the last one. "	35, 36, 38, 43, 44, 46, **48**, 53, **54**, 68, 72, **83**, **84**
⇜ "... to get a tutor."	**38**, 56, **83**, **84**
⇜ "... to decide what to major in."	38, 42, **63**, 64, **82**
⇜ "... to figure out what classes to take."	**38**, **56**, **82**
⇜ "... help."	**38**, 54, 55, **56**, 65, **Chapter 7**
⇜ "... a better way to study."	**41**, 43, 44, 48, **53**, 54, 72, 84
⇜ "... to get organized."	**47**
⇜ "... to stop studying with the wrong people."	24, 51, **52**
⇜ "... more friends."	**56**, 60, 62
⇜ "... more motivation to study."	26, 27 **59**, **64**, 67, **72**
⇜ "... to have some coffee."	71, 72, **74**
⇜ "... to stop drinking so much coffee."	71, 72, **74**

Student seems to be having a hard time...	RELEVANT TOPIC PAGES
❧ ... completing their homework.	**24**, 26, 31, 33, **37**, 63, 65, **72**, 73
❧ ... sustaining study sessions for an adequate amount of time.	24, 25, 26, 27, **31**, 33, 35, 53, 59, **71, 72**
❧ ... staying awake during class or study sessions.	26, 27, 35, 62, **71**, 72, **74**, **76**
❧ ... maintaining a good study schedule.	32, **33**, **34**, 37, 65
❧ ... putting enough time into a course because it doesn't seem relevant to their major or career.	34, 37, **63**, 64, **67**
❧ ... arriving to class or meetings on time.	**33**, 65
❧ ... remembering everything they've studied.	32, **34**, 41, 43, **44**, 45, 53
❧ ... going to class.	34, **36**, 41, 43, 44, 45, 53, **63**, 65, 71, 76
❧ ... succeeding in their courses.	35, **38**, **56**, 63, 67
❧ ... maintaining academic confidence.	42, 60, **66, 68**
❧ ... answering essay questions on tests.	**43**, 45, **48**, 53
❧ ... taking effective notes.	41 , **44**
❧ ... building connections on campus.	**38**, 54, **56**, 60, 62
❧ ... taking personal responsibility for overcoming setbacks.	38, 56, 59, **61, 65**, 67, 68
❧ ... seeing the long term benefits of persisting towards graduation.	**63, 67**, 82

Student mentions...	RELEVANT TOPIC PAGES
◦ ... studying in bed or in front of the TV.	**23**, **24**, 25, 71
◦ ... that they listen to music while studying.	**27**
◦ ... cramming for a test.	31, **32**, 33, **34**, 37
◦ ... pulling an all-nighter.	31, **32**, **34**, 37, 74, **76**
◦ ... studying past midnight.	31, **32**, 33, 37, **76**
◦ ... focusing all of their time and energy on only one course.	**37**
◦ ... trying to start a new nutrition plan or sleep routine.	**35**, 41, 62, 64, 71, **76**
◦ ... having missed class.	**36**, 67, 76
◦ ... interest in seeking academic assistance like tutoring or advising.	**38**, 54, 56, **Chapter 7**
◦ ... having test anxiety.	**45**, 81, **83**
◦ ... getting off-task with friends while studying.	**51**, **52**, 71
◦ ... wanting to get more socially involved on campus.	54, **56**, 60, 62
◦ ... failing to turn in homework or submitting substandard work.	**37**, 67
◦ ... problematic or upsetting personal life circumstances.	38, 56, 59, 61, **65**, 68, **73**
◦ ... interest in attending graduate school.	63, 67, **82**

Student struggles with...	RELEVANT TOPIC PAGES
❧ ... getting to bed on time.	35, 65, 71, 74, **76**
❧ ... staying focused during study sessions.	**24**, 25, 26, 27, **31**, 32, 52, 59, 65, **71**, 72, 74
❧ ... resisting social influences to neglect homework.	24, 25, **52**, 63, 71
❧ ... remembering the appropriate material for a test.	26, 34, **45**, **48**
❧ ... knowing that they have an academic problem, but being unable to identify a specific source.	**65**, 82, 83
❧ ... time managment.	**33**
❧ ... writing papers.	**81**, 84
❧ ... reading the textbook.	**26**, 27, 31, 34, **37**
❧ ... seeking help when it's needed.	**38**, 54, **55**, 56, 68, **Chapter 7**
❧ ... knowing how to approach the material of a particularly hard course	**41**, 43
❧ ... maintaining academic self-esteem.	42, **66**, 68
❧ ... notetaking skills.	41, **44**
❧ ... performing as well on the test as on their homework.	45, **48**, 72
❧ ... negative thinking.	27, 33, **59**, 60, **61**, **65**, 68
❧ ... blaming others.	**61**, 68

Student suffers from...	RELEVANT TOPIC PAGES
❧ ... a lack of long-term goals.	63, **64**, **67**, 68, 82
❧ ... not having the motivation to start and sustain study sessions.	**24**, 27, **31**, 35, 37, 59, 63, 67, 71, **72**
❧ ... not having enough energy to engage in effective study sessions.	26, 35, 37, **59**, 65, 71, **72**, 73, 74, 76
❧ ... erratic variations in their test and homework scores (both high and low).	35, 38, 45, **48**
❧ ... distracting periods of sleepiness, hunger, or irritability.	24, 31, 35, **62**, 71, **72**, 74, **76**
❧ ... insufficient academic progress.	38, 54, 56, **63**, **67**, 82
❧ ... academic insecurity.	42, 45, **66**, **68**
❧ ... surface learning, where only the most basic concepts are grasped.	34, **43**, 46, 54, 63
❧ ... poor notetaking skills.	41, **44**
❧ ... test anxiety.	**45**, 48
❧ ... poor organization skills.	**47**
❧ ... unsupportive friends who criticize the student's academic involvement.	52, **56**
❧ ... lack of sleep.	35, 62, 74, **76**
❧ ... poor motivation.	26, 35, 38, 56, 59, 62, **63**, 67, **71**, 72
❧ ... difficulty adjusting to campus life.	38, 55, **56**, **65**, 82, **83**

Student feels...	RELEVANT TOPIC PAGES
❧ ... bored with the course content or homework.	**53**, 54
❧ ... that they have more work than they have time to complete.	26, 31, **33**, 37, **65**, 72, 77
❧ ... that attending class is optional or unimportant.	**36**, 34, 63
❧ ... lost.	38, 55, **56**, **64**, 65, 68
❧ ... discouraged or overwhelmed.	27, 42, **56**, 60, 61, 63, **65**, 66, 67, 68, 71, 72, **83**
❧ ... less equipped for college than their classmates.	**42**, 47, 54, 61, **66**, 67, **68**
❧ ... tired or groggy.	35, 71, 72, 73, **74**, **76**
❧ ... rushed when taking exams.	34, **45**, **48**
❧ ... dismissed by their instructor's behavior.	55, **61**, 68
❧ ... disillusioned about the benefits of staying in school.	**63**, 64, 68, **82**

Study Simpler Progress Tracking Sheet

STUDENT / GROUP NAME _____

PAGE	TOPIC	DATE DISCUSSED
23	STUDY SPACE: Place Cells	
24	STUDY SPACE: Avoiding Distractions	
25	STUDY SPACE: Relocation	
26	STUDY SPACE: Productive Ambiance	
27	STUDY SPACE: Music & Mood	
31	STUDY INTERVALS: Take a Break	
32	STUDY INTERVALS: Review Often	
33	STUDY INTERVALS: "Personal Time Survey"	
34	STUDY INTERVALS: Engram Maintenance	
35	STUDY INTERVALS: Tracking Progress	
36	STUDY INTERVALS: Course Attendance	
37	STUDY INTERVALS: Homework and Reading	
38	STUDY INTERVALS: Seek Resources Early & Often	
41	STUDY METHOD: Individual Differences	
42	STUDY METHOD: Multiple Intelligences	
43	STUDY METHOD: Bloom's Taxonomy	
44	STUDY METHOD: Notetaking Skills	
45	STUDY METHOD: Managing Test Anxiety	
46	STUDY METHOD: Active Listening	
47	STUDY METHOD: Organizational Skills	
48	STUDY METHOD: Fluency and Speed	
51	STUDY PEOPLE: Introversion vs. Extraversion	
52	STUDY PEOPLE: Social Influence	
53	STUDY PEOPLE: Teach to Learn	
54	STUDY PEOPLE: Supplemental Instruction	

PAGE	TOPIC	DATE
55	STUDY PEOPLE: Get to Know Your Professors	
56	STUDY PEOPLE: Building a Community of Support	
59	STUDY LOYALTY: Having a Positive Attitude	
60	STUDY LOYALTY: "The Hidden Power of Smiling"	
61	STUDY LOYALTY: Victim vs. Creator	
62	STUDY LOYALTY: Maslow's Hierarchy	
63	STUDY LOYALTY: Atkinson's Model of Motivation	
64	STUDY LOYALTY: Motivational Styles	
65	STUDY LOYALTY: Motivational Barriers	
66	STUDY LOYALTY: Grow Your Intelligence	
67	STUDY LOYALTY: All Diplomas Look the Same	
68	STUDY LOYALTY: Fixed vs. Growth Mindset	
71	STUDY ENERGY: Glucose & Self-Regulation	
72	STUDY ENERGY: Fuel Proper Study Habits	
73	STUDY ENERGY: Uncertainty and Energy Levels	
74	STUDY ENERGY: The Myth About Coffee	
76	STUDY ENERGY: Sleep	
77	STUDY ENERGY: Dreams	
81	STUDY RESOURCES: Writers' Center	
81	STUDY RESOURCES: Disability Support Services	
82	STUDY RESOURCES: Career Services	
82	STUDY RESOURCES: TRiO Advising & McNair	
83	STUDY RESOURCES: Counseling Services	
83	STUDY RESOURCES: Tutoring	
84	STUDY RESOURCES: khanacademy.org	
84	STUDY RESOURCES: Online Tutoring	
84	STUDY RESOURCES: Academic Software	

References

Introduction
Starting Simpler

1 student. 2013. From Merriam-Webster.com. Retrieved November 8, 2013, from http://www.merriam-webster.com/dictionary/student

2 Tinto, V. (2012). Completing college: Rethinking institutional action. University of Chicago Press.

3 Gardner, H. (2004). Changing minds: the art and science of changing our own and other people's minds. Harvard Business Press.

Chapter I
Study Space

1 O'Keefe, John, Nadel, Lynn (1978). The Hippocampus as a Cognitive Map. Oxford University Press.

2 Gailliot M., Baumeister R., DeWall C., Maner J., Plant E., Tice D., Brewer L., & Schmeichel B. (2007). Self-control relies on glucose as a limited energy source: willpower is more than a metaphor. *Journal of Personality and Social Psychology, 92 (2)*.

3 Munch, M., Linhart, F., Borisuit, A., Jaeggi, S., & Scartezzini, A. (2012). Effects of prior light exposure on early evening performance, subjective sleepiness, and hormonal secretion. *Behavioral Neuroscience, 126 (1)*.

4 Hedge, A. (2004). Linking environmental conditions to productivity. *Power Point presentation*. Cornell University.

5 Moss, M., Cook, J., Wesnes, K., & Duckett, P. (2003). Aromas of rosemary and lavender essential oils differentially affect cognition and mood in healthy adults. *International Journal of Neuroscience, 113(1)*, 15-38.

6 Birren, F. (1997). The Power of Color: How It Can Reduce Fatigue, Relieve Monotony, Enhance Sexuality, and More. Carol Publishing Group.

7 Husain, G., Thompson, W. F., & Schellenberg, E. G. (2002). Effects of musical tempo and mode on arousal, mood, and spatial abilities. *Music Perception, 20(2)*, 151-171.

Chapter II
Study Intervals

1 Cepeda, N., Pashler, H., Vul, E., Wixted, J., & Rohrer, D. (2006). Distributed practice in verbal recall tests: A review and quantitative synthesis. *Psychological Bulletin, 132(3)*, 354-380.

2 Cepeda, N., Pashler, H., Vul, E., Wixted, J., & Rohrer, D. (2006). Distributed practice in verbal recall tests: A review and quantitative synthesis. *Psychological Bulletin, 132(3)*, 354-380.

3 Dunlosky, J., Rawson, K. A., Marsh, E. J., Nathan, M. J., & Willingham, D. T. (2013). Improving students' learning with effective learning techniques promising directions from cognitive and educational psychology. *Psychological Science in the Public Interest, 14(1)*, 4-58.

4 Sio, U. N., Monaghan, P., & Ormerod, T. (2013). Sleep on it, but only if it is difficult: Effects of sleep on problem solving. *Memory & Cognition, 41(2)*, 159-166.

5 Time Management. (2007). Retrieved November 26, 2013, from http://caps.gmu.edu/educationalprograms/pamphlets/TimeManagementBro_7-07.pdf

6 Semon, R. (1921). The Mneme. London: George Allen & Unwin.

7 Liu, X., Ramirez, S., Pang, P. T., Puryear, C. B., Govindarajan, A., Deisseroth, K., & Tonegawa, S. (2012). Optogenetic stimulation of a hippocampal engram activates fear memory recall. Nature, 484(7394), 381-385.

8 Landsberger, H. A. (1958). Hawthorne revisited: Management and the worker, its critics, and developments in human relations in industry. *Cornell studies in industrial and labor relations, 9.*

9 Chen, J. and T. Lin. (2006) Class attendance and exam performance: a randomized experiment. Society of Labor Economics (SOLE) Eleventh Annual Meetings, May 5-6, 2006, Cambridge, MA.

Chapter III
Study Method

1 Dunlosky, J., Rawson, K. A., Marsh, E. J., Nathan, M. J., & Willingham, D. T. (2013). Improving students' learning with effective learning techniques promising directions from cognitive and educational psychology. *Psychological Science in the Public Interest, 14(1)*, 4-58.

2 Gardner, H. (1985). Frames of mind: The theory of multiple intelligences. Basic books.

3 Armstrong, T. (2009). Multiple intelligences in the classroom. Association for Supervision & Curriculum Development.

4 Bloom, B. S., Engelhart, M. D., Furst, E. J., Hill, W. H., & Krathwohl, D. R. (1956). Taxonomy of educational objectives: Handbook I: Cognitive domain. New York: David McKay, 19, 56.

5 Dunlosky, J., Rawson, K. A., Marsh, E. J., Nathan, M. J., & Willingham, D. T. (2013). Improving students' learning with effective learning techniques promising directions from cognitive and educational psychology. *Psychological Science in the Public Interest, 14(1)*, 4-58.

6 Mark Gilbert and Karen Gilbert. Test Anxiety PDF.

7 Peterson, R. [iSpeakDotCom]. (2009, March 30). Russ Peterson explains why active listening is difficult [Video file]. Retrieved from http://www.youtube.com/watch?v=CPDQgaDiDJE

8 Reiss, S. (2008). The normal personality: A new way of thinking about people. Cambridge: Cambridge University Press.

9 Dunlosky, J., Rawson, K. A., Marsh, E. J., Nathan, M. J., & Willingham, D. T. (2013). Improving students' learning with effective learning techniques promising directions from cognitive and educational psychology. *Psychological Science in the Public Interest, 14(1)*, 4-58.

Chapter IV
Study People

1 Estabrook, M. & Sommer, R. (1966). Study habits and introverstion-extraversion. *Psychological Reports, (19)*.

Chapter V
Study Loyalty

1 Isen, A. M. (2002). A Role for Neuropsychology in Understanding the Facilitating Influence of Positive Affect on Social Behavior and Cognitive Processes. Handbook of Positive Psychology. Oxford University Press: Chapter 38: 528-540.

2 Gutman, R. [TED]. (2011, May 11). Ron Gutman: The hidden power of smiling [Video file]. Retrieved from http://www.youtube.com/watch?v=U9cGdRNMdQQ

3 Downing, S. (2012). On Course. Cengage Learning.

4 Cox, Valerie. (nd.) The Cookie Thief. *A Matter of Perspective.*

5 Engler, B. (1991). Personality theories: An introduction. Houghton Mifflin: 359-368.

6 Atkinson, J. W., & Reitman, W. R. (1956). Performance as a function of motive strength and expectancy of goal-attainment. *Journal of Abnormal and Social Psychology, 53(3)*, 361.

7 Reiss, S. (2002). Who am I?: The 16 basic desires that motivate our behavior and define our personality. Penguin.

8 Gatewood, J. D., Morgan, M. D., Eaton, M., McNamara, I. M., Stevens, L. F., Macbeth, A. H., ... & Kinsley, C. H. (2005). Motherhood mitigates aging-related decrements in learning and memory and positively affects brain aging in the rat. *Brain research bulletin, 66(2)*, 91-98.

9 Blackwell, L. A., Trzesniewski, K. H., & Dweck, C. S. (2007). Theories of intelligence and achievement across the junior high school transition: A longitudinal study and an intervention. *Child Development, 78*, 246-263.

10 Dweck, C. (2006). Mindset: The new psychology of success. Random House.

Chapter VI
Study Energy

1 Mischel, W., Ebbesen, E., & Zeiss, A. (1972). Cognitive and attentional mechanisms in delay of gratification. *Journal of Personality and Social Psychology, 21(2)*: 204–218.

2 Gailliot, M. T., Baumeister, R. F., DeWall, C. N., Maner, J. K., Plant, E. A., Tice, D. M., ... & Schmeichel, B. J. (2007). Self-control relies on glucose as a limited energy source: willpower is more than a metaphor. *Journal of Personality and Social Psychology, 92(2)*, 325.

3 Van Tulleken, A. (2014). One twin gave up sugar, the other gave up fat: their experiment could change your life. *MailOnline.com*. Retrieved January 30, 2014, from http://www.dailymail.co.uk.

4 Alquist, J. L. (2010). What you don't know can hurt you: Uncertainty depletes self-control resources (Doctoral dissertation).

5 Rogers, P. J. (2007). Caffeine, mood and mental performance in everyday life. *Nutrition Bulletin, 32 (1)*, 84-89.

6 Trockel, M., Barnes, M., & Egget, D. (2000). Health-related variables and academic performance among first-year college students: implications for sleep and other behaviors. *Journal of American College Health, 49(3)*, 125.

7 Reddy, S. (2013). The perfect nap: sleeping is a mix of art and science. *WallStreetJournal.com*. Retrieved September 2, 2013, from http://online.wsj.com.

8 Wamsley, Tucker, Payne, Benavides, & Stickgold (2010). Dreaming of a learning task is associated with enhanced sleep-dependent memory consolidation. *Current Biology, 20(9)*.

Chapter VIII
The Tutor Guide

1 Bandura, Albert (1986). Social Foundations of Thought and Action: A Social Cognitive Theory. Englewood Cliffs, NJ: Prentice-Hall.

2 Bandura, Albert (1997). Self-Efficacy: The Exercise of Control. New York: W. H. Freeman.

3 Bandura, Albert (1997). Self-Efficacy: The Exercise of Control. New York: W. H. Freeman, 79-115.

4 Tobin, K. (1986). Effects of teacher wait time on discourse characteristics in mathematics and language arts classes. *American Educational Research Journal, 23.*

5 Duell, O. K. (1994). Extended wait time and university student achievement. *American Educational Research Journal, 31.*

6 King, A. (1993). From Sage on the Stage to Guide on the Side. *College Teaching , 41 (1)*, 30-35.

7 Fisher, D., & Frey, N. (2008). Better learning through structured teaching: A framework for the gradual release of responsibility. ASCD.

8 Vygotsky, L.S. (1978). Mind and society: The development of higher psychological processes. Cambridge, MA: Harvard University Press.

9 Tuckman, B. (1965). Developmental sequence in small groups. *Psychological Bulletin, 63 (6)*: 384–99.

10 Bradshaw, J. (1972). A taxonomy of social need. *New Society, 30(3)*, 72.

About the Author

My initial interest in the field of education occurred in 2003 during a Learning & Teaching Concepts class taught by the consummate Merrilee Webb. I was particularly struck by the work of Howard Gardner, whose inspirational theories galvanized my interest in both education and psychology. While I was majoring in music at the time, Merrilee encouraged me to consider switching my major to psychology: "You don't need a degree to be a good musician," she said, "but you *have* to have a degree to be a good psychologist."

Her advice has served me well. Since completing a bachelor's in Psychology and Music in 2007, I have enjoyed the privilege of remaining employed in the field of education, with an emphasis on psychological aspects of learning and instruction. My primary roles during the past seven years have been as a tutor and program coordinator, but, upon the completion of my master's degree, my continued interest in the field of educational psychology also provided me with opportunities to teach and to write *Study Simpler*.

Currently, I work and reside in the city of Cheney, Washington, home of Eastern Washington University, where I enjoy continued involvement in education, working with both students and a staff of 60 wonderful employees. My wife and I share the joys of raising three children. None of my accomplishments would be possible or meaningful without the devotion and support of my wonderful wife, Courtney, whose contributions to this project have been essential to its progress and completion.

Special thanks to Gail Forsgreen, Aaron Brown, Theresa Davis, Verlinda Washburn, Carlos Munoz, Lindy Tinker, Lauren Dimock & Mark Roberts for being inspirational examples and providing me with feedback and support.

www.studysimpler.com

CPSIA information can be obtained at www.ICGtesting.com
Printed in the USA
LVOW02*1502110414

381357LV00003B/3/P